For more than thirty years I have enjoyed the privilege of speaking and singing Keith Harrison's words in performances in Australia, England and both North and South America. I never have more confidence of being able to reach and enthrall an audience than when I am performing this poetry. The evocative power of his language works for me in the same way as that of the great bard.

It is a poetry that must be spoken aloud; its musical quality is akin to the line of a fine melody. Even rugged children that I have taught over the last twenty years would frequently come to me in the schoolyard and say, 'Do us another one of those poems sir.' I knew what they wanted, it was either one of Keith Harrison's poems, or one of the Shakespeare speeches. This new and wonderful volume speaks for itself, as do the poems and songs and stories it contains.

— *Geoffrey D'Ombrain*

Keith Harrison's **New and Collected Poems** is a major achievement. Among contemporary poets in English he is the one whose skills seem to come closest to those of a good novelist. He creates memorable characters. At the same time, his descriptive writing is subtle and rich. He can invent telling epigrams ('How many one-legged soldiers have marched for two-legged kings?' or 'Jealousy .. can catch/The creak of bedsprings, clear across five counties'), but he is at his best in creating complete worlds. See how more and more deft touches are added to the initial brushstrokes, in the supple rhythms of *Winter Canticle*:

> Look at the red fox sliding under the wind
> Belly-fur riffling the swamp's green hair;
> A squeak of ground-plovers, wings
> Clapping about her head, and always
> The swivelling wind with its thousand smells...

Both Australia and the USA can be proud to have helped form/inspire such a wide-ranging poetic mind.

— *Mark O'Connor*

I challenge anyone to find me a living poet as good as Keith Harrison. Highly educated, he is also a child of nature. He knows the known poetry of the world and yet belongs to no school. He has given himself the freedom to compose poems about the wilds, as well as about settled life. He can write about childhood or war, about workers and idlers; about the twist in the heart or about transcendence — never losing the poetic craft he acquired first in his native Australia, and then in England. Later, Keith Harrison found leavening in the land of Whitman and Melville.

— *Molly Daniels Ramanujan*

Here is God's plenty — love poems, laments, songs written to music, portraits, dramatic monologues, chants, haiku, georgics, narrative poetry. I know of no other contemporary poet with the range and depth of Keith Harrison. If you buy just one book of poetry this decade, buy this one.

— *Jane Taylor McDonnell*

I first entered Keith Harrison's world with *Orchard Poems,* some of the best of which I am delighted to find collected here in CHANGES. His work succeeds on multiple levels and his voice does the fine work of 'chipping a flint,' offering images and deliverances full of a keen light that cuts to the heart of the matter. It is a rare pleasure to have these poems in one place. His voice is important, his themes and images diverse and forceful. Keith Harrison's work honors that good place in ourselves, while warning us to be wary of any ideology that asks us to surrender our individuality. I come away from this collection with the sense that, as he puts it in 'Lions, etc,' I have also known 'riches beyond my deserving.'

— *Susan Thurston Hamerski*

This collection represents Keith Harrison's last forty years of 'thinking hard about sound' (as he puts it in a recent poem), 'the shuttle of live syllables'. His syllables live in the ear and the pharynx; and they resound in the heart's mind with earthy music, rhythmic and remarkably good humored. They thrum with melodies both sweeping and jagged, with harmonies now angular, now lush, as they speak of mother earth, her signs and seasons, calling to us, reckless offspring, who live out our lives upon her. Thus these verses, new as they are, show an ancient quality: bardic, vatic, pulsing to a basic beat.

— *Jackson Bryce*

Harrison's seriousness as a poet lies not only in his dedication to skill but it is also found in the pith of his subject matter; the fact that while an entertaining portion of his poetry has a humorous, even skittish bent, on the whole he chooses to deal with the bone of life . . . This collection reveals the range of his work. It cannot be associated with a contemporary trend or attached to a particular school. It is distinctly individual. Many of the poems achieve that instant of recognition, that bond of respect and friendship which readers share with the verse that they re-read. CHANGES is likely to be a well-thumbed book.

— *G.B.H. Wightman*

Keith Harrison is an important poet. He is thinking, challenging, beady, eclectic, inventive, dramatic, playful, aphoristic, tender, passionate, always extremely skilful; above all, his poems glow with a huge generosity of spirit. This really substantial New and Collected Poems, the work of forty years and more, should not only win him wide-spread admiration but also love because, time and again, his poems nudge the heart and print themselves indelibly on the mind.

— *Kevin Crossley-Holland*

[Keith Harrison] knows all about the necrotic mess we have made of our world. He is saved from despair by his powerful lyric gift. He dives through the stinking wreck, never missing a thing, and comes back with brilliant, redemptive images of friendship, deep learning, nature, love, places and things. Now we can read him the way he should be read, a lot at a time, the poems working on each other as we read, feeling the gathering up of force, the giving off of that hard-won glow that makes our lives bearable. He is right up there, in this, with Hopkins and a few others.

— *Wayne Carver*

CHANGES

New & Collected Poems
1962-2002

Keith Harrison

with 15 prints by Karin Calley

BLACK WILLOW PRESS

northfield

© *Keith Harrison, 2002*

ISBN NO: 0-939394-13-8

Cover design by Mark Heiman
Reeds, Gunderbooka by Jenny Gibson
Author's photo by Rob Morrow
Interior illustrations: 15 prints of plants of the Australian southern tablelands
by Karin Calley

Printed in 11 pt. Bembo by Lightning Source

Permission to use poems from this book, save for short quotations in reviews and articles, must be gained in writing from the author and **Black Willow Press.**

ACKNOWLEDGMENTS

Many of these poems have been published in my previous collections: **Points in a Journey** (Macmillan, London, and Dufour, Pennsylvania), **Songs from the Drifting House** (Macmillan, London), **The Basho Poems** (The Nodin Press, Minneapolis); **A Burning of Applewood** and **Words Against War** (Northfield, Black Willow Press) and in the following magazines, newspapers and periodicals: *The Age* (Melbourne), *Aquarius* (London), *The New Statesman, The New York Times, The Atlantic Monthly, Poetry Northwest, The Piedmont Literary Review, Poetry Singapore, Southerly, Island, Meanjin, Overland, Quadrant, The Prairie Schooner, The Great River Review, Ironwood Magazine, The Carleton Miscellany, The Scotsman, The Australian, The Toronto Telegram, The Canberra Times* and *The Geelong Advertiser.* Some have been re-printed in these anthologies: *Australian Poetry, 1961, '63, '65, '66; Borestone Mountain Poetry Awards, 1964; Young Commonwealth Poets, 1965; Australian Voices; Two Centuries of Australian Poetry, 25 Minnesota Poets, The Oxford Book of Contemporary Australian Verse, Plain Songs (Seven Carleton Writers), Plain Songs II* (Northfield, Black Willow Press), and *Around Geelong.* Individual poems and translations have been broadcast on the B.B.C. (London and Bristol) the A.B.C. Sydney, Radio India, WSUI (Iowa City), WCAL (Northfield) and Melbourne Community Radio. My thanks to the respective editors and publishers for permission to re-print them here.

Throughout my writing life I have been sustained by so many people that it would be impossible to name them all. The following people have been a constant inspiration: Philip Martin, the late A. K. Ramanujan, and Kevin Crossley-Holland, who have all helped in so many ways; my daughters, Katrina and Rebecca, and my former wife, Christina Harrison; Elizabeth Edwards, Liz Lupien, Jim and Jane McDonnell, Judy Daniel, Bob Tisdale, Jackson Bryce, George and Carolyn Soule, Molly Daniels Ramanujan, Nancy Soth, Liz Ciner, Beth McKinsey, Chiara Briganti, Alvin Greenberg, Seamus Deane, John Daniel, George Wightman, the late Paul Ritchie, John Gulbrandsen, Susan McKinstry, Frank Morral, Robert Drummond, Wayne Carver, Robert Edwards, Jane Spiro and Mark Heiman. For help with the translations from Rilke I am indebted to Richard Hornung, from the Japanese to Michael Kelsey and from the Russian of Pushkin to Diane Nemec-Ignashev. Jenny Gibson has read, re-read and proof-read most of what's in this book over a period of almost five decades. Without her firm counsel and judgment this book would have been much the poorer.

An early draft of this collection was begun, and many of its poems written whilst I was staying at my second home at Pirra Arts Centre, Lara, Victoria, where Jenny Abella and my friend, Geoffrey D'Ombrain were my hosts for more than a decade. Geoffrey D'Ombrain not only commissioned a good number of these poems for performance with the Pirra Arts Ensemble, but has been a source of sustaining energy for almost half a century. There is no adequate way to thank him, nor all my other friends, colleagues and fellow writers for their gifts of the spirit.

for
Philip Martin
and
in memory of
A.K. Ramanujan

Say Yes *to change, live in the fire of change;*
In that fire you'll find more change, and more —
Be inventive, a spirit that flies out of range
And delights at the foot that spins on the dance-floor.

If your only fuel is yourself you're already a stone.
Nor can you flee into grayness, nor choose to stall.
Why? Because when you're withdrawn and alone,
Over your head a huge hammer's poised to fall.

Let go, open out, be a spume of knowing that flows
Through a country of dreaming vineyards, and wolves,
Whose end's a beginning just when it comes to an end.

Your spirit will stand there amazed, wherever it goes
By the children of parting — like Daphne's, whose flesh dissolves
Into laurel, and who wants you to change into wind.

After 12, Part II, Rilke's *Sonnets to Orpheus*

Foreword

This book gathers all the new poems and all the poems from my previous collections that I want to keep at this stage. As I look back over more than forty years of writing the story takes a different shape, one that a chronological arrangement doesn't capture. It seemed to me sensible in this collection to arrange the new poems and the old ones in groups where they belong together generically. So I have re-ordered many of the poems in the previous books and let them rub shoulders with their brothers and cousins: all the songs are now together, all the dramatic monologues, all the shorter translations, and so on.

Yet there is a chronology of sorts, and it forms an arc. I have begun with two new collections and an adaptation of some lines from Virgil completed in 1997, then swung back forty years or so; then ended the book with **Snail-Tracks**, another group of poems composed mainly in the '90's.

★

As I have lived, and written, in two different language-cultures — English-speaking, and American-speaking — there is a certain deliberate and somewhat necessary inconsistency in the spelling in this book. It seemed to me sensible that for poems written in or about America I should write *'plow'*, not *'plough'*, *'traveling'* not *'travelling'*, *'color'*, not *'colour'*, and so on. Similarly, for poems written in or about Australia and England, I have used so-called standard English spelling. Experience tells me that American readers are not much bothered by alternative spellings, and I hope my English and Australian readers will be equally tolerant. My own view is that spelling matters much less than the intended meaning, but perhaps not everyone will agree.

In a few cases I have made some emendations, mostly minor, to poems previously published elsewhere.

Hackbery Hollow, Northfield, Minnesota
Pirra Arts Centre, Victoria
Canberra, A.C.T.
1996–2002

CONTENTS

BROWN MUSIC, New Poems 1993–2002
Past Sixty-Five by a Month or More, 11
Vita: Minnesota Fall, 12
Birthday Numbers, 13
Builders, 14
Dogwood, 16
Hawk on a Burnt Pole, 17
At Ouray, 17
Angle, 18
A Kind of Love Poem, 19
Black Water/Blue Wind, 20
Wayne Comes Back from Utah, 21
For Raman, 22
For Rolfe, Coming Home, 24
A Little Midnight Elegy, 25
Love Poem, After Heavy Snow, 26
Winter Canticle, 27

WORDS AGAINST WAR, 1990–1996
In my Freshman Year, 33
Legs, 34
General, 35
Man with a Phone, 36
Field-Notes for the War Against England, 37
Wedding-Song, 44
The Bees, 46

SONG OF THE EARTH, after Virgil, 1992–1996, 49

from POINTS IN A JOURNEY, 1966
Points in a Journey, 65
Autumn Afternoon, with Birds, 70
A Mild June Day, 70
Refusing Song, 71
Detail of an Estrangement, 72
Two Spanish Pieces:
Morning Music, 73
Late Summer, 73

Sleepless in Florence, 74
Contraries: December, 75

THE WATER MAN, A Narrative for Voices, 79

PORTRAITS, MASKS & MONOLOGUES

PORTRAITS
Uncle Jack, 101
Two Women, 103
A Man Dead, 104
Colonel Cheeseman's Commencement Party, 105
The Ecstasy of Karmstad Karleson, 107
Lines for a Teacher, 108
So Quietly, 111
Single Handed, 112
A Hot Day In Kansas City, 113
North, 115

MASKS
Lovers, 117
The Island Weather of the Newly Betrothed, 118
Song of a Lecherous Man, 119
Married Song, 121
An Invention, 122
Fourteenth Honeymoon at the Cameron Hotel, 123
The Surf at Whitnaby, 124
Man in the Train, 126

MONOLOGUES
Piero, Painting, 127
Song from a Play, 127
Olof Andersson's Rune, 128
At the Edge of Winter, 129
Wife Waiting, 130
Australian Tongues:
Barracoutta Fisherman, Tasmania, 131
Opal Miners, 132
Post-Graduate, 133

Dentist at Work, 134
Leichardt in the Desert, 135
The Hired Man's Retrospect of Winter, 136

ORCHARD POEMS *1976–1991*
A Burning of Applewood, 143
Dawn in California, 145
Dung Beetle, 146
Ballad, 147
The Sense of Falling, 149
Last Evening, 150
Not Quite Ithaka, 151
Summer Poem, 153
Young Bears in an Orchard, 155
Here, 155

Poems from **SONGS FROM THE DRIFTING HOUSE (1972)**
The Fallow Season, 161
Blizzard, 161
A Word in December, 162
Two Variations on a Ground, 162
Nine for a Wasp at Lunchtime, 164

COLLECTED SONGS
Songs of Lara & the Bellarine (1997)
Geoffrey, 173
A Widow of Wild Dog Creek, 174
Old Ted, 175
Francesca, 176
King of the Gallery, 176
The Winemaker's Winter Song, 177
Three Chants for Voice and Didjeridu:
Rock Lizard, 178
Wave Cave, 179
Ceremonial Song for the Cleansing of the Wind, 180

Four Songs for Children, *182*

Six Little Songs on Time, *184*

Two Popular Songs, *185*

Songs from the Drifting House, *187*

Jim Busby's Rune at Cider Time, 190

A Town and Country Suite, 1978
The Japanese Windbell's, 191
Hanging Pigeon, 191
A Warm Day in January, 192
Blizzard, 192
Bob Broderson's Song of the Wheel, 193
As the April Sunlight, 194
Song of the Central Tree, 195

THE BIRDS AT PIRRA, 1987
Kookaburra Kanon, 201
White-Faced Heron, 202
Cockatoos, 203
Brolgas, 204
Magpies, 205
Macropeus Giganteus:
(1) He carry no wings, 206
(2) And Now they Graze at the Edge of Time, 207

WHITE WAVE, 1974–1978, *211*

TRANSLATIONS
The Squatters, After Rimbaud, 229
After Pushkin, 230
After Rilke, 230
Transatlantic Version of Rimbaud's 'Ma Bohème', 231
Two Poems by Théo Léger:
Tomb of an Apostle, 232
A Single Tree, 232

Under the Lime-Tree, After von der Vogelweide, 233
After Francis Jammes, 234
'Correspondances', After Baudelaire, 235
For Hélène, After Ronsard, 235
Street Crossing, After Tomas Tranströmer, 236
After Gerard Duval, 236

From the Japanese:
Three Love Poems, 237
The Masters of Haiku, 237
Spring Poems from the Kokinshu, 240
Autumn Poems from the Shin Kokinshu, 240
After Buson, 241

THE COMPLETE BASHO POEMS

THE BASHO POEMS (1972 & 1981)

BASHO BESIDE THE MOUNTAIN
Basho Beside the Mountain, 249

THE THING DIRECT
Reply to the Grammarians, 253
Hangover Poem, 253
Quick Shadow, 253
Sketch for an Aesthetic, 254
He Recapitulates/Forecasts the Stages of his Life, 254

HIS TRANSMIGRATIONS
Traveling Toward the Vache Qui Pue River, 256
Basho Rejects Hinduism, 257
Happy Day Among the Elephant People, 257
The Sage Who Came By, 257
He Rebukes His Underwear, 258
Late Breakfast, 258
The Crocodiles Who Stayted Too Long, 258
Railroad Tanka, 259
Minnesota Winterdrive, 259
Basho in Melbourne, 259
SEVEN DREAM POEMS, *260*
BASHO DEVISES HIS OBITUARIES, *262*
AN INTERVIEW WITH BASHO, *264*
from BASHO'S 81 POEMS ON THE MOODS AND MODES OF THE PIGEON, *269*
Notes on The Basho Poems, *285*

★

WHEN THE IRISH BULLS ROLLED OVER, *287*

BASHO PLAYS GOLF, 293

SUBJUNCTIVES
and Poems Previously Ungathered
Revenge, 305
Kids, 306
Pleasures, 307
Seven Thoughts on Poetry, 307
Pirra in Deep Winter, 309

A Gift for My Daughters, 310
Before the Blizzard, 311
Falling, 311
Wedding Song, 312
Questions for Oenone, 312
Not Thinking Now, 313
Words for *The Immigrants, 314*
Otters at Battle Lake, 316
Being Here, 317
Quarrel, 318
Great Masters, 319
Scribbled in the back of The Origin of Species . . , *321*
In Small, 322
A Chain of Saws, 324
Elegy for a Staring Boy, 325
Approaching Minneapolis by Car, 325
Red Fox in Winter, 326

SNAIL-TRACKS, *New Poems 1993–2002*
Thank You, Pythagoras, 331
Seriously, 332
Hands, 334
Caroline, 334
Even Stevens, 336
Cousin Jock, 336
Justice Barrie and His Mistress, 338
At Supper, Not Where He Eats, 339
Leavings, 341
Catullus in a Datsun, 342
T-Shirt Poems: The Seven Seasons, 344
Wimmera Snake-Time, 346
Lions, etc., 347
Mother and Dad at Ninety-Three, 351
Profondeurs at 2.a.m, 353
Snail-Tracks, 354

Notes on the Poems, 357
Index of Titles, 360
Index of First Lines, 365

BROWN MUSIC
New Poems 1993-2002

PAST SIXTY-FIVE BY A MONTH OR MORE

And it must be the thirteenth snowfall of the year breaks like flak through the river-willows
And the big barn rocks on its keel like a tramp-ship nosing into a storm
Hurling a spray of ice-seeds at the windows of my study.
I have cleaned my house but there's no joy in that as the days blow away
Like so many puffs of thistle-down. Box-elder bug on its back, I wave my legs in the air
And the woman on the video cajoles me: *Make sure you do this every day.*
So I ride my bicycle, mile on mile, and never move, and row
Red-faced across the floorboards but reach no shore, only a rock-band
Booms as the rowlocks in my backbone squeak and I know whatever holds me in
It's not the winter.
      Why do I choose this trade, and choose again? These words,
This paper-thin ice of meaning which cracks with the lightest touch and we fall in,
                 and drown.
We run words through our brains like whippets, train them to fetch in hell,
Believe and disbelieve, old obsession; with words we damage our friends and lovers.
What am I doing bending over my desk again? Chipping a flint that someone,
Later, might strike a flame? — when all the time I know that Heraclitus had it right:
All is flux and snow: you hardly have time to scratch your signature when a truck
Plows through your windshield or the valves in your heart freeze up, and all that hot
Presumption you call your self whites out, and your children look amazed
At your empty T-shirt dangling from a hanger.

I am trying, while there is time, to put my words in order. So many notes,
So much unfinished, I want to get some right, I want to show my daughters at least,
Look — out of all this I have shaped one thing clean and firm, but I stare at my scribbles,
Then plunge outdoors into the snow-surf, and stare at my tire-marks vanishing
By the mail-box, at the mad smoke swirling from my neighbor's chimney
And cannot think of any rightness that comes with age, and keep on hoping that beyond
The foolishness and blindness there is something like joy, which today seems frozen,
A flower drowned in crystal.
         Then I remember the bloodhounds:
How they can follow us days beyond death because every one of us sheds fifty thousand
Microscopic flesh-flakes each second that we breathe. But what comfort,
While this bitter snow-wind thumps the trees to know that, with so many
Million legacies each day, when we at last shut down, we will persist for a week or so
In ghostly grains — tiny snowstorms to twitch the nostrils of a hound?

Raman's gone, and Dinny O'Hearn, and George, and lately, Keith, and Paul, and more,
                                                                              and more,
And I am angry with my friends, and grieving: their passing leaches our lives away.
                                                                              In the mouth
Of death and snow, I want to shout a spiteful song, but there is only this wind,
                                                                              this breathing

Until I think of an old man, twenty years beyond me, who smiled on all of us
And sent us home, ashamed of our vanity and fears, when he stiffened his back
And the voice, breaking through phlegm and pain, like an old warrior's
Bursting backward into youth, declaimed, *I am not done*, and, Stanley,
I take your words and give them back, knowing you will forgive my theft
As the voice of the snow-wind howls across the barn, and I am standing now
My head in fire, and remembering, and singing with you, and singing again
And again, *I am not done with all my changes.*

For Stanley Kunitz

VITA: MINNESOTA FALL

Because my father told me, *No*
I pitched my will against the blow
Of his flint mind and angry heart.
Almost four, I began the art
Of silence and of cussedness.

When I was seven, with a curse
And a kindling-stick he whacked my bum
Till my pants flushed with a wet flame.
The sun chilled, leaves hung dumb.
I called out. No one came.

Because my mother told me *Yes*
Before I read them in a book
I guessed her reasons by her look,
And soon I learned that there were rules
Older than rocks, not taught in schools.

The jacaranda bloomed: a blue shout,
Louder each year, till I got out
And took to wandering, wanting to fill
My days with words, and work of hands.
Now, as I sense my slide downhill,

Half-finished projects clutter my desk:
A bricolage of clips and bands.
Fall gives off a peculiar musk;
Leaf-rot mixed with the stink of coons
And turkeys: mildewed afternoons.

The days get stranger: two friends die,
One in his garden, one in bed.
Smelling of pee, our fathers lie
Staring at nothing, or coil up
In a tight ball over a coffee-cup.

All things have their tides and reasons:
People and trees, and these queer seasons
Between two countries where I'm home
Nowhere and everywhere. As I turn
Gripping my hammer in my palm,

To patch the familiar roof and walls
Of my house, of my self, what's gone
Seems chaff in the wind. I'm on my own:
One with the coons and, I suppose,
With turkeys, and the browning rose.

Be that as it may, night spreads.
It spreads fast. I hurry outdoors
And shift my ladder along the wall.
Testing each rung, I begin my climb
Through deep doorways between the stars.

BIRTHDAY NUMBERS

Sixty-five, soon sixty-six:
The years vanish like burning sticks

BUILDERS

My father
Taught me the ways of
Knots and tools;

He showed me
How to whip a rope
With an old

Marlingspike
He'd salvaged from his
Years at sea.

He'd tuck the
Loose whippings under,
Pull them firm

And the frayed
Ends would tighten, stiff
As a stick.

Almost with
Awe he'd touch the tongues
Of chisels

And jackplanes.
He loved the feel and
Tang of wood.

His plane hissed
Down the long oak-grain
Spinning thin

Shavings up
Through the sun-shafts in
His workshop.

Then he'd squint
Down the plank, muttering
To himself.

He taught me
All the knots he knew,
And they are

Beautiful:
Sheep-shank, Garrick bend,
Clove hitch — all

Their forms like
Fluent signatures
Each with its

Character
And purpose. I
Practice them

Now, with my
Grandson, Nicholas.
He's four. We're

Working-men
Taking a breather.
I wonder

If he'll learn
These old disciplines
Although, as

For the knots,
I rarely use them — yet,
When we were

Lost last month
In a black sea-storm
My clove-hitch

Held the mad
Sweep-oar we rigged to
Turn us home.

The tools, though,
Are a different thing.
I keep them

Oiled and honed:
Imperatives from
My father.

Ninety-four,
His handgrip still like
Carbon steel,

I call him
For his birthday: Ten
Thousand miles.

Good-day, there,
He says. *Still got it?*
                  'What?'
That knife

*I lent you
Last year. Still use it?*
'Yep'
         Good. Keep

It sharp, now.
'Don't worry. Hone it
Every day.'

He tells me
He plans to build a
Boat with wings

To lift planes
Downed at sea. He thinks
Of the dead.

'Terrific,'
I say, 'Send me all
Your sketches.'

I hang up.
We're lying about
The knife. That

Was '60,
Maybe '61.
I lost it

Moving house,
Somewhere in England.
We both know

I'll never
Find it now.
          A man
Who touched words

Sparingly,
He told me: '*Tools are
The point where*

*Geometry
Meets nature: always
Difficult;*

Respect it.'
That was his own, and
Almost worth

The years of
Solitude, the pain
He never

Shook away.
With respect, I hand
My grandson

His hammer
And we both bang nails
Hard into

The big house
We're building in the
Cedar-fork

With the birds
And spiders. I watch
His face as,

Frowning, he
Concentrates, and I
Remember

The clear blue
Gaze of my father —
At four, and

Ninety four.

DOGWOOD

Ice on the wind and three hawks
Tuning the thermals with black wings.
Look below:
Flames of sumac splinter
And dance across the field.
But in the bones of the dogwood row
The fire remains:
A stubborn energy that stains
Them licorice-red all winter.

Now, a blind midwinter spring
Quickens their sap: three days.
The bones blaze
And at their ends tiny buds
Are quivering.
What can we imagine that will stay
Precise?

You say
They want their sudden green, then
Their crimson brilliancies.

Then nothing.

All this, you say, *again and again.*

Desire, desire: it is impossible
To think of a world with no
Desiring mind.
                But not
A mind like ours, which stutters
Before these spikes of blood that
Strike so fiercely
Out of the sleep of snow.

HAWK ON A BURNT POLE

My wings fester with light,
One by one, my ash-feathers fall.
As my body fizzes into nothing
I hunch myself together. Who wants to be
Last bird, bone-dust on a pole, rubbed
By a sulphur wind that slides over dead farms?

Years ago I watched oil-slick
March up the beaches, cocooning seal-pups
And gulls in a smooth death, that shone.
This one flared, five days, then chilled;
Cities blackened, lakes boiled.

Weeks from now, from Jupiter they'll see
White pustules of light across the continents.
When will the secret written in my cells
Dance in the woods again?
My throat hardens, my eye
Witnesses nothing that cries or moves.

AT OURAY
for Joel and Diane Kramer

What are the high crows telling us
As they flash their wings up there
Like bars of flexed obsidian,
Then vanish,
Leaving in the amethyst air
Two tiny specks of sound?

ANGLE
for Peter Raven

Pearl-shell light
Over the lake as
I wind through

Michigan
North of the Big Thumb.
Early dawn.

My mind is
Heavy, all the farms
Are sleeping.

To my left,
Deep pinewoods, flickers
Of aspen,

Mile on mile;
Cuts for power-lines,
Loggers' roads.

Further on,
Clearings, with corn, beans,
Alfalfa.

The lake's edged
With water-weeds, snarled
By waves that

Can hurl dead
Trees across the road.
This half-light's

Tricky. Watch.
One man in a car.
You're not here,

Where poisoned
Eagles turn inland
Breeding less

Each year, where
Cormorant chicks,
Bills bent, can't

Crack their shells,
And neutered lake-trout
Never spawn —

You're not here
To remonstrate but,
Exactly,

As your gifts
Allow, to see things
As they are.

Cease railing.
Think what to do. Think
Very hard.

A horned moon
Flares among nacreous
Cloud-swirls, then

Full dawn, with
Long salvos of light.
My car pumps

Ruin on
Everything that's green.
I am one

With this lake
Which rots with our greed.
I share this

Journey with
You, in an age of
Extinction.

Seen from the
Moon, the mighty lake's
Only a

Shoreless blur.

A KIND OF LOVE POEM
For a Blind Musician

Hearing your absence now in every room,
The black mouth of the piano open but un-singing,
Impatient with the difficulty of words,
I bang the window-ledge
And startle the grackles in the hackberry tree.
They fly off, carking, to my neighbor's maples.
I laugh, and breakfast by myself in a patch of sun;
Then plunge into the day and punch five nails
Deep in the cedar plank, and feel them
Bite home. I check the level, bounce on the steps.
Everything holds.

Now, in a fume of crushed apples, with your kind of clouds
Riding over, I taste the satisfaction of being alone;
These limits, these particulars: a few leaves
Balanced on brown grass-tips, the log-pile
Ready for the saw, and the brilliant house
Drifting on its emerald sea.

What is it that I honor with such good blood
Around the heart this morning? Ah, it is something
Clean and lively, something in you:

> *Each mortal thing does one thing and the same . . .*
> *Selves — goes itself . . .*
>   *For that I came.*

And I rejoice that you stand there in
Your separateness, your mind brimming with music:
Not the evasion but the transformation of pain.

And I honor all that springs
From what, in our double dark,
We touch together, as we move
Down into this new winter, keeping our edges sharp,

Honest as wheat, and lucky as the river.

BLACK WATER / BLUE WIND

For Geoffrey & Nick D'Ombrain

Out early. Just as we round the channel buoy
A storm kicks up from nowhere. We reef
The mainsail down till it's only a boom
Swinging above our noses. Faster than we can shout,
It's night at six a.m. White wave-tips
Thicken to a surf that bucks the stern. We drive
Down, and hold on, then rise, flailing
About for stays and taffrails. Wind
Clear astern, we ride the water-hills
Like a skier, lights on the land gone out,
Sea hurtling under us pulling, tight-lipped,
Starboard, starboard, to keep our bearing, then
As we heel, the tiller-shaft snaps, the rudder's
Swinging free. We rig a sweep from deck-boards.
It jumps out of the foam and snarls against the hull.
Now we're driving downwind fast, 10 degrees
Then 35 off-bearing. The youngest, a boy of twelve,
Calls out over the wind: *'It's okay to die,
As long as it's interesting.'* In darkness we agree.

More than an hour like this, a sea-bird planing,
Waiting for a shoal to snap the keel, then
Like a horse through a plate-glass window, we burst
Into the sun, and in a broad moment, the sea
Simmers and falls.   Now there are only
Buffets of blue wind shaking the sail
And sliding over our faces.
                              Only blue wind,
But now that our hands are quiet again,
Like a sour guest returning for his hat,
The memories, scared off by the storm
Come back, the lies and the betrayals:

They find you once again in the same tense
Kitchens and hallways, their syllables
Hot in your mouth, you cannot
Spit them away. You try to drown them
But they are like torpedoed sailors
Black with oil-slick, who refuse to drop
Their heads among the sea-wrack.
       So it has come
As always, to a game of stealth among
These hesitations of wind and water.
We trim the sheets, we hold on hard
While the taut sail drags us back to land
Back to our untidy selves. Back home.

WAYNE COMES BACK FROM UTAH

Wayne comes back from Utah with dark stories:
The belly of an old friend swelled so fast
In a little week his days had come to nothing:
Hardly had time to scratch his name. And tells
More stories: uncles and cousins, all gone, taking
Voices from the kitchen, taking long fields with
The *thwock* of baseballs, *and all of them so quickly.*
Darn it, it takes your breath away. He tries to laugh.

I remind him of the dapper man of eighty
Who told me, over coffee in this room
Of the last days of his wife. *I had a happy marriage.*
Now, living on my own, I'm busy, busy,
And mostly joyful. Wayne says nothing.

I remind him of the Buddha's advice
To the young mother mourning her only child.
Walk through the village, knock on every door,
Find me a house where death has never visited.
When she returns she admits: *Master, I found no home*
Where death has never been.
       Wayne drops his gaze.

With, lately, so much dying for both of us
I'm whistling in a gale. *Seems a whole battalion*
Of broken ones is stumbling toward a cliff — and we
Not far behind. We both go quiet. This is our village.
And we're becoming strangers. Young faces with
No names stare at us from familiar tables.
                                                                Outside,
A big rain jumps and smokes along the sidewalk.
We're old gaffers a little fuzzy of hearing.
Someone's turned off the music.
It used to be all around.

FOR RAMAN

Who gave mouth-to-mouth to the drowning
And revived them over a thousand years
By breathing with their breathing;

Who gave us, when he spoke,
So many worlds with their pulses and colors
That the air about him became

A thunder of wings, the piss-tang
Of ripe jackfruit, an old pig snorting
In a country jakes and he, the small boy

Staring down;
                    Whose every speech
Proved that, when all the cerebral furies
Fall away, it is only poetry, time and again

Can go unflinching among skulls,
Betrayals, the silence of God
Or the silence where God might be;

And taught us, this being so,
To weigh each phrase, as if
Our friends' lives hung from our exactitudes —

And all this lightly, lightly,
Like Mozart with his billiard balls.
A certain impishness

A certain fastidiousness, a detachment —
And, beneath all that,
Something indestructible, clean as a diamond.

This morning, the air alive with wrens,
And the must of dropped apples,
I strode into my house, and found him there

Deep in a book, in his usual place
By the fire and, looking over his shoulder,
Heard his voice rise from the page, with its lilt

Of reverence and candor, and I knew once more
He would never leave this house. He has become
Our spirit of the hearth, companionable,

Completely human.

In Memoriam, A.K. Ramanujan, 1929–1993

FOR ROLFE, COMING HOME

When all your choices tightened about you
And you knew that you must walk a narrowing
Path between tall trees, alone, you left
Your city of glass and metal sunlight
And with the sureness of a fox, came home
Where all the voices spoke one language,
Spreading around you
Like dawnlight over quiet water. And still
Your gaze kept the same detachment as, when a child,
You studied us, tilting back on your chair, with impish
Curiosity and humor. You always had our measure.
Then, as your body fell away, you deepened
As if you were hiving in yourself
Some mellifluous, secret thing,
Nourishing, and solitary as Mozart
Who walked beside you every day
On your unthinkable journey.

To the last second, until you could breathe no more,
Your courage and your dignity were inviolable.

That was the gift that you bequeathed yourself.
Now, almost nonchalantly,
You have handed them on, to take into our care
As best we can: these stubborn, human things
That spill across our endings and our beginnings.
Now, wherever we walk, we will carry you
With us, lightly, seriously,
Until we also falter. Then, as we have honored
Your gifts, we will pass you on.

*Read on Saturday February 12, 1994, Skinner Memorial Chapel,
Carleton College at the Memorial for Rolfe Tisdale (1960–1994)*

A LITTLE MIDNIGHT ELEGY

Chopin winding down again
                Vin Buckley's gone
                                  too many
        Fifteen below

Lovely, the dark snow
   covering the house

                and Marion bleeding
        in a room, high over Naples

not blood, but something else, you see it
                falling from her eyes

                        Why, once again
    do I think of my pimpled youth,
                        and Helen

  who wound a scarf of light about my days?

  and Jenny gone, and Paul
  with a brutal suddenness
                        too many

Five blessings on us all

                    Whom have you loved?

  Britt, certainly,
            back straight as a broom, who kicked
     the nonsense away
                              Elizabeth
      her roguish heart still 'dansand merrie'

Lovely, the dark snow
tumbling in the lilacs
                    It's cold, it's late

    Vin's gone, rewind the Chopin

       tomorrow and tomorrow

These beings in our blood, these echoes

                Lovely, the dark snow
                   covering our eyes.

LOVE POEM, AFTER HEAVY SNOW

Two whole days, in white explosions,
Stars hurled their frozen fragments down
Then, last night, the sky became black wine,
The stars hardened and
We lunged outdoors and dug, hour on hour
And found the hulk of a car, engine stuck,
Doors ice-welded to its body
Like wings of a giant beetle. We banged
And cursed and breathed on it
And, just at midnight, made it
Rise and roar.

      And all the time, arms swinging,
      I thought of you, and the hot snakes
      Watching from the bracken.

Last night I came to my senses:
Love is right now or not at all.
We burn in snowdrift or in stubble,
Limbs heavy with life in the slow
Urgency of noon or midnight, time
Still, but always running and, throats hot,
We filled three flagons and drank them down
And told loud stories round the fire, and laughed,
And climbed the stairs to sleep

      Thinking of you — a smudge
      Of watercolor haze on the hills, creekwater
      Singing.

I have known you so few days
And so many days my arithmetic unravels.
Sometimes, especially when water speaks
Under the ice, our thoughts cross,
Or when the big tree shakes itself and
Basketsful of new snow tumble down.

I peel my glove away, and rub my hand
In the mystery of snow.

Now, with every restless body
Gone from the house, except my own,
With starlight caught in the icicles,
I think of you once more
As they drip their minutes down
In intervals too fast or slow
For me, or the night, or anyone to know.

WINTER CANTICLE

Look at the red fox sliding under the wind
Belly-fur riffling the swamp's green hair;
A squeak of ground-plovers, wings
Clapping about her head, and always
The swivelling wind with its thousand smells:
Cow-dung, clover, a man there
Sweat decaying in his overalls, tobacco
Staining the air between; and he
Will blast you away like smoke from his mouth
And blast the skunk and the sparrow-hawk, take life
From anything that moves against his corn-row.
What's left he'll hang on a fence to dry.

Keep low and away, keep sliding beyond his eye-beam.
Soon the treacherous light will crumble
To cavern-dark, pups yipping against your flank
And the moon staring down with its single eye.

★

Out there, beyond the headland, the tanker hog-rolls
In a scud of foam and fog, carrying black death from the sun
To ram into the mouths of a million seals, death sluicing
Under her hatches, and the crew climb over her like ants
Obeying the green language of her computers.
And she, giant larva, lunging through the swell
Having the power to punch holes in the sky, goddess
Of slag and burnt-out cities, it is her voice
Whistles through the rusted derricks of lost mining towns:
Sudbury, Walhalla, Eldorado,
Through thistle-heads in the cracks of factory walls,
Over sea-hulks and the shells of lorries.

★

If we believe that life is merely body,
This hunger, this foraging, and the bitter gifts of age,
The goddess will also drag us down.
                              There is a different
Energy endures beyond these slate-eyed men
Conspiring in beetle-black cars. The Greeks
Knew it well and found it
In the dry vinestock that quickens every year
With new sap under the pruner's hands.
This is the stubborn thing, the force that
Overflows our obituaries. How quickly the dogs of death
Forget that the green world is what we imagine
And lose, and prove again, and will imagine.

★

When we come home to the good place in ourselves
There's a brown music like the hum of bees,
And then the speech of our hands is delicate and sure;
We touch our children and our aging fathers.
This greeting, this farewell, the cantus firmus
On which all our smaller songs depend.

We stand here in the courtyard in winter sunlight,
Carried a moment beyond the edge of speech
Carried to a place where sound rises in quiet columns.
Clumps of pampas push up from the ground,
Like the heads of giants, our witnesses.

The Greeks are in us and the green bones of our children.

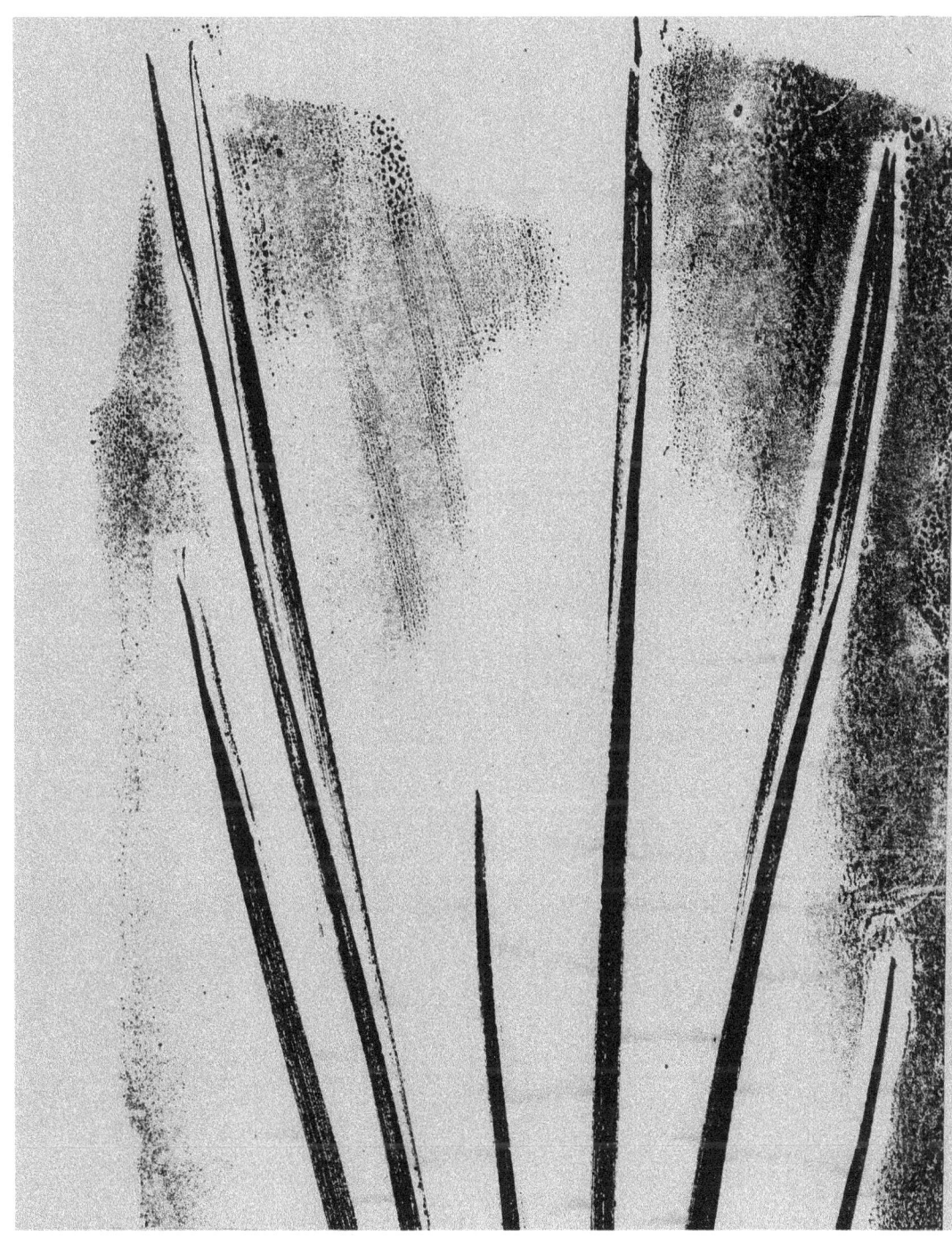

WORDS AGAINST WAR
1997

IN MY FRESHMAN YEAR

In my freshman year the fury of Vietnam
Broke out, and we woke up in hell. I remember
A gathering in Great Hall, late September,
Where three young men rose up, each with a story
That deeply questioned the old, unquestioned tag:
Dulce et decorum est pro patria mori.
Their voices steady, they accepted their task,
Their sentences complete, knowing the risk,
They spoke out, then struck a match and burned the cards
Which ordered them to march beneath a flag
And offer up their lives for another's words
And the flames in their hands replied: *Non serviam.*

Standing beside the president of the College
I studied his face: he was concerned, then suddenly proud
That three young men, be they right or wrong,
With such clean manliness, though they be flayed
By parents, teachers, and an ignorant throng,
Should so resist. I was young. Those men were in my charge.
My head was crammed with another kind of knowledge;
They would soon be vilified for theirs, but they were large
In spirit, and they would not be cowed
By those who reproached them with unthinking zeal,
For they had found their center, and it tasted real.
I thought them unimpeachable. That is why I stayed.

Read at the Opening Convocation, Carleton College, Sept. 10, 1993

LEGS

For my students

How many one-legged soldiers have marched for two-legged kings?
Look at them hopping across the screen, black suits
Pressed for Remembrance Day, medals from Vimy Ridge and Passchendaele
Banging against their chests, and the film jumping to the rhythm
Of their crutches. There are enough to fill five cities;
And even on single legs they keep faithful step, eyes fixed as bayonets
Dead ahead.

How soon they forget that the king has dressed himself in a score
Of counterfeit uniforms all bloodied now, and stiff, under a song of flies.
Meanwhile the king, in a long frock and feathered hat, surveys the campaign
From a distant manor, advisors swirling around him
With maps as he smoothes the expensive silk
Along his thighs.

At this, and any time, not to be paranoid
Is highest foolishness. This executive, whose eyes
You cannot see behind his brilliant lenses, will never hack your hands off;
He will take what dreams in you on the twentieth floor at coffee-break —
The part that shapes a tune for your flute, or bends a clay bowl
To the exact form of your delight — and he will tweezer it out of you
Very slowly.

See them milling there in the quadrangle, these youngsters
Ready to be crippled for someone else's dream of excellence
Which carries them to a high apartment above the wrinkled river,
An apartment blank as Hotspur's eye as he stares up at the cold clouds
Riding over.
                    And everywhere the young pretender struts,
He builds his kingdom on the skull-bones of his father; and once
At twilight, alone in the royal ante-room, he slips the crown
Over his curls, listens to his father's sick breathing
And smiles into the mirror.

His name is Hal, and he is everywhere.

Watch him, I tell you.
Go well downriver, build a small shack on the tidal flats
Camouflaged like an egret's nest so the black
Patrol boats can't pick you out with their long
Eye-beams at midnight.

Hunker down, be suspicious of any communiqué which offers
Terms for your surrender.

GENERAL,

Some day, after your kind, you'll die
Between clean covers, dreaming of perfect battles,
While those who gave flesh to your abstractions
Had their guts blown out in the sand, or legs
Snapped up behind their backs, asking
For a last cigarette from an orange-seller,
A bearded man (like me), also dying because
Of oranges, and bombs, and an open sky.

Rommel was a courteous man, and blind;
Like you, he placed his body on the line;
Like yours, his political brain was smaller than a prune.
Both born to fight, not cavil on a hair.
For deeper cause we have to look beyond you —
Not into the eyes of Kali, or under the cloak of Sin,
Or into that most futile place of all,
The argument from *Human Kind*.

How many pieces of silver, slipped through subtle hands
So that our guns could swivel against us? We had trusted
In thought. Now, in the desert of your minds
All shrivels to the dialect of Lombardi:
Winning is the only thing. Throw in *Love* as well.
I sometimes think you'll all stand up in hell
And cry: *We have come to release you;*
Whistle our anthems and fire at our commands.

If you fall first, this is what I shall say:
General, I'm sorry they're taking you out
With geraniums and Vivaldi. You did not fool about,
You fought: *Not like those chicken-shit*
Intellectuals! I shall remember how you flayed
The press: *Our boys are **not** out here to fight for oil!*
On that you'll never go back, as you said to a friend:
Ebullient, tough, and ignorant to the end.

General, I will not rise for you. Instead, I stand alone,
Puttering, confused, your shrapnel in my mind,
Asking: *When the smoke clears, what have we won*
Besides your victory?
                              The cancer is that zeal
And we have found no cure. Your moon-face smiles
Down on the world. *Flags, burnt bodies.* We turn you off.
Now we must try, once more, the difficult thing:
We must inch forward in a time of stone.

MAN WITH A PHONE

. . .We go along, sometimes for decades, believing that in some fundamental sense everything is more or less O.K. — that the commonwealth is in relatively good hands. Then, one day we realize that a thing of such enormity as war, say the Gulf War, begins behind someone's eyes. Someone who says: *Yes, start the bombing. We will probably kill thousands of the enemy, and maybe some of our own men. But I have calculated the risks and gains. Start the bombing.*

Someone with his ear against a telephone, a man with indigestion and an unresolved family problem, a man who has been brushed on occasion by the wing of his own death, a man with a frown in his brain. Somewhere in the buzzing of his synapses he makes a decision: for certain purposes, such as the continuity of oil-supplies and other reasons, much more vaguely defined, he concludes that it is necessary to kill people.

On the same day his cousin makes a decision, also in a place behind his eyes, to buy cheap land for a toxic waste-dump in Louisiana. It flourishes and brings fatal disease to the neighborhood. Many of his own countrymen die, some very slowly. He knew that would happen. While the war flares in the sands of the desert and thousands of innocent people are bombed, he practices his putting. His handicap is down to five . . .

FIELD-NOTES FOR THE WAR AGAINST ENGLAND

Prospero: *He does make our fire,*
Fetch in our wood, and serves in offices
That profit us. . . . .

★

Cal.   *You taught me language and my profit on't*
Is, I know how to curse.

                                 The Tempest

I have come
Once more to London,
Now, in a

Time of war.
Three slow nights I have
Walked the streets

Of London
Past wolf-men sleeping
In tunnels

Underground
Dreaming of Grendel,
The cold stars

Of April
Churning above me.
In the sands

Of Iraq
The armies gather. The
Announcer

Clears his throat,
The clock clicks forward
By degrees.

★

I lunge out
Into the night, my mind
Sick with a

Strange fire. There,
In the wastes I find
My kinsman

Caliban,
Misshapen ward of
Prospero,

His mother,
Sycorax, a hag:
Imperial

Fable that
Fits well. He tells me
He can speak

Now, tells me
He was a fine butt
While the play

Ran, but now
Prospero's done with
Him, what then?

We walk on
Avoiding every
Lighted hall;

We walk on in
Silence, dreaming
Of black fire.
★
Another
Fable turns this way:
My forbears,

You remind
Me, came from dank hulls
Moored in their

Own stench on
The silver Thames, two
Sickening years,

Thrown there for
Snaffling rabbits, or —
Their kids crazed

With hunger —
Bits of bread. Hundreds
Rotted while

Waiting for
A Whitehall jackass
To decide:

*'Virginia —
Or Botany Bay?
No matter,*

*Ship them out —
They're too expensive!
Ship them out!'*
★
The story's
Half-wrong, but it will
Suffice for

A century:
A convenient
English lie:

It keeps thought
Lost in a haze of
Sherry-fumes.
★
This England
This museum, where
Bats twitch their

Wing-tips in
The sour air, and the
Queen snores in

Her old tomb
Dreaming of a lost
Imperium.
★

These sudden
Castigations flare
From an old

Hurt I've not
Told before: I'll set
It down flat

In my way:
For twenty years now
I have held

My doors wide
For you, and since I
Am only

Half-welcome
In your land, I have
Turned away

With Grendel,
Caliban, mastering
My own tongue

In this strange
Country where bloodless
Lions peer

From scutcheons
Whose growls are only
Bat-pipings

Echoing
Through dusty halls and
Corridors.

★

Churchill's next:
Who better for an
English text?

Libya,
Burma, Malaya:
All of those

Betrayals.
Our fathers told us
Otherwise,

But the facts
Burn like mustard-gas
In the eyes

And the lungs
Of live men — your
'*Tropical*

Guinea-pigs.'
The record's in their
Blackened flesh:

And those cliffs
Where my uncle died;
Turkish guns

Cut him down
As, with his mates, he
Ran at them

Row on row
For England, cut them
Down like wheat

In the name
Of a doddering king.
Meanwhile

On the beach
With their binoculars
The fat farts

Of England
Watched the slaughter and
Drank Pimms.

Cut
To Changi:
Churchill's bungle, right
From the start.

Oh, yes, your
Boys were taken too.
But never

For us. Ours
Died for you in sand
And jungle,

Meanwhile, the
Japanese navy
Scanned our shores.

Churchill raged:
*We need you now in
Malaya;*

*The Empire,
The honor of the
Empire.* We

Refused. He
Raged on: *Australians!
Fools, cowards!*

Churchill, for
You, was next to God —
For us, a

Brandy-swilling
Blimp with a sharp tongue
Duping us,

Once again,
With fealty to
A cracked crown.

★

I sailed here
Forty years ago
Looking for

Origins
And I have found that
What we need

Is a scour
Of flame against our
Fathers' words:

That nonsense
That politesse — all
That is suave

Tight-assed and
Condescending.
    This
Is my song

For Abos,
Welshmen, wops and boongs
Scottish gits,

Muslim sods
And Anzacs — all who've
Eaten dung

Under the
Flag of Prospero —
For Oxford

Indians
Who ape their masters'
Tricks and tropes

Revering
Fools like Everest
Who flattened

A hundred
Villages to keep
His map-lines

Straight — for spades
And fuzzie-wuzzies,
Cockney geeks,

Pakis, Jew-
boys and Irish dogs,
I have come

Back to say
I am declaring
Mental war

On England.

(Convict Song: Botany Bay)

If only we had some boxes of tea
Like our mates in Boston town
But Georgie's got us by the cods,
Everything's battened down.

Three broke out from Macquarie Bay
And only one returned
He'd eaten his brothers on the way —
Jesus, our stomachs churned.

Pick a padlock and sweat in hell,
Piss on the Governor's tree
They'll chuck you to the sharks in the swell
While the Governor sips his tea.

Bromley escaped to Borneo
(Yes, Borneo) they sailed him back;
He tried again, but this time home
Trussed up in a gunny-sack.

I'd like to hang that sodding runt
Who at floggings gets a hard-on,
That holy man with starch on his neck
The Reverend Samuel Marsden.

★

The best of
Friendship is the death
Of fear and

Anger, when
The bitch of the world
Stops biting

When, in the
Space of noon, hunger
Falls away:

When beer foams
In long glasses and
Yeast-smells climb

Your nostrils
Mingling with leaf-rot
And mown hay.

A bright bird,
A cardinal, flicks
Through the trees,

And is gone:
These moments in the
Realms of day.

We have been
Brothers many years,
We carry

So many
People in the house
Of our minds

All of them
Hungering to stand
And sing. There's

Hrothgar, and
Arthur, and the mad
Banjo-man

From Memphis
Who kept us laughing
Till first light;

There's blind Jack
And the Opal King,
And Seamus —

A flood of
Voices, such frayed nets
To hold them.

★

The lesson
From loss is learning
How to mend.

I have walked
The streets of London
In a time

Of war, my
Mind pitching against
These granite

Conundrums
Of our history:
Loyalties,

Betrayals;
Scuds over Baghdad.
Our screens flare:

Images
Of rockets, dead tanks,
Gutted planes.

This is the end
Of empires; dry sand;
Flies, and dreams.

★

A wolf-man
Deep in the underground
Stirred from sleep

And banged his
Fist against his box
And coughed hard,

And twisting
Toward me with red eyes
Out of some

Whiskey-hell
Said nothing, only
Glared at me,

And I thought
For a mad second
As I gazed

Up the piss-
ridden stairs that we'd
Never climb out

Of this to
Sing again.
     Above us,
World blacked out,

Time dragging
Us backwards, away
From the sun.

WEDDING SONG
for Katrina and John

Your walking here has made no sound at all.
It had the sureness of a signature,
An exactitude of water-drops, or crystals
Glistening in a thunder-egg:
                                    these footfalls
Down the aisle, this walking which
From now, we shall call Katrina and John
Came from its own quietness to this door
Which none, beside you, can see, though we gather round
While you pause together on its threshhold.

And now the ghosts come crowding in.

If you listen lightly beyond your breathing
You will catch the skirl of bagpipes, and the thrum
Of wooden drums and, now and then, the silver
Sound of a kantela rising in a smokey hall.
You will also hear rough seafaring men
Breaking bones on an iced beach; there are times
When our cells remember everything: such
A charged thunder of benedictions in the air.
These beings have come to encircle you
And bless, as we, the living bless:
John and Katrina, Katrina and John.

I have flown back from England
To make this wedding song for you
In a time of war, when hope and anger
Cross in flares on our horizons,
And we have found that wars have their beginnings
In a place more terrible than the nothing
Between the stars, and closer than the blood
Throbbing behind our eyes.

This is a difficult thought, and true
Here, in this chapel on your wedding day.

Because you have chosen this, your day,
And because the ghosts of our mothers and fathers
And the ashes of soldiers are trying to speak
Here in this chapel
Let us give them our courtesy
So that the quietness that brought you here
As the speech of the guns falls away
Can echo again, and again, with theirs.

Your walking here has made no sound at all.
It is as if, by simply walking, you have found the way.

Now everything waits. Here is the door. Go in.

Katrina Harrison & John Strot, Carleton College Chapel, February 2, 1991

THE BEES

What came of fire was fire
And then, more fire, singeing the desert air
Sick-orange and sunset-red a hundred days.
What came of fire were hordes
With computers, wading in ash
Designing new campaigns:
A supersonic hatred, a sash
Of violence, tightening everywhere.

Our eyes are bloodshot from the flares.
Who robbed the time of sleep?
Dry insects scratch at the corn-husks
But find no sustenance. The wind that blows
Our farms away comes from a deep
Hole in ourselves, a hole we carry as we
Hurl our bodies about between stars
And when we lie down flat, as in our graves.

I told myself this is a time
For mending and for peace, a time for
Coming home. I had been walking
An hour or so, quarreling with all I knew,
A quarrel to no end. Stuck in despair
I stood. Then, heading in, I chose
The track that led by the barn, and there
Rounding a curve by the broken bridge
In the narrow space between two wars
I came to a stop in long green shadows
Amazed by the music of the bees.

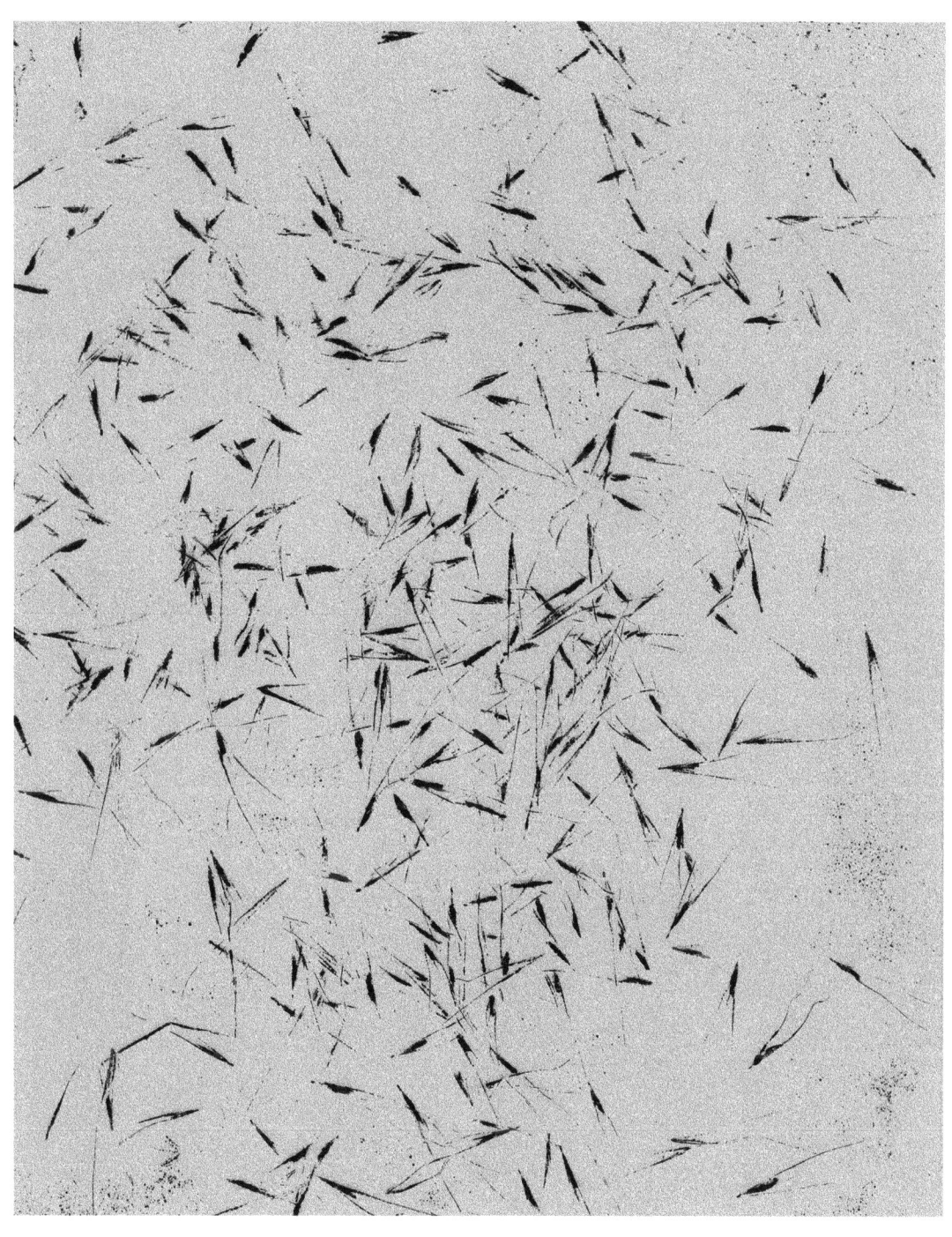

SONG OF THE EARTH
After Book 1 of Virgil's Georgics

for Jackson Bryce
of course

What makes your corn shoot high, when's the right time
For plowing, how to make your grape-vines
Intertwine like lovers on the boles of elms;
How to raise healthy cattle, and live your life
Without waste, in harmony with your clever bees —

All that, old friend, is what I'll tell you now.

Sun and Moon, you great lamps who draw
The years across the sky so quietly;
Mother of grains, who evolved, from
Scatterings of acorns, wide fields
Of corn and wheat and barley; and you,
Patron of mirth and darkness, with wine-fumes
In your whiskers as you stroll among
The clustering grapes, changing pale
Springwater into yeasty must; and all you
Tiny beings whose speech we hear
In barn-shadows and puffs of flying thistle-down,
Be with me now as I compose my song.

I think I can hear you dancing there,
Or is it in my blood that you are moving
Now, as I think of you who, with your three-pronged fork,
Struck earth and produced a field of stallions,
And you, old man of the woods, with your puckered face,
For whom the cattle are grazing all around? Small god
Of flutes, whom I have loved since boyhood,
Come out of hiding once again and make your fingers skim
The woodland scales; patroness of olive-groves, young giants
Of the plow, guardians of the forest who pull up trees
And set them down in crumbling river-banks —
All powers that crack rocks and make them flower,
And send shuttles of white rain across our fields;

And last, you august persons who climb the Capitol steps
Whether your name resound in time like a god's
Or be engraved, mid-ocean, on all our maps,
Whether it be fixed forever on some undiscovered
Galaxy, way out there between Scorpio and Virgo,
Listen: our land is sick with greed. Whatever
Time makes of you, and all your counsellors,

Stand by me now in this new enterprise,
And share my concern for uninstructed farmers
So that, come what may, you will prove
Larger than your ambition, and the hags
Of death will never drag you down.

ψ

In first spring,
                    when black ice slides
Down the hillsides and
                    runnels of snowmelt
Drench the fields,
                    when earth softens
And the west wind gets up,
                        that's the time
To be busy with your plowing;
                        then, long furrows
Scour the plowshare clean.
                        Only crops
Twice warmed by sun,
                      twice chilled by frost
Will satisfy the hunger
                      of the farmer
Never-satisfied,
                    and fill his barn till the walls
Burst, and his bins
                    overflow with grain.
But remember,
              you have to scan
The winds, read
              all changes in the weather;
For each field keeps
                a spirit of its own:
One place is best for crops,
                        one for setting
Young vine-stocks;
                  another likes apples, or
A patch of forage-grass.
                  The facts endure:
Some dry hill-slopes
                  are saffron country,

Particular valleys
                are homes for barley,
Alfalfa, or hay;
                 these rocks house copper;
Those, veins of iron-stone.
                        And how rare
Those special stud-farms
                that breed, year
Upon year
        race-winning lines of mares.
These certainties have stood since mankind sprang
Out of a world which, then, was nothing but stones.

ψ

Knowing all that,
                begin your first-month's plowing.
Turn the damp sod,
            let it bake in the low sun.
That checks the weeds from
                  choking early corn.
If the clods are dry,
            when Venus brightens
Turn the earth over in
              shallower furrows
To hold the moisture in —
                or your field is a pan of dust.

ψ

Let new-cut fields go fallow, rest them
A year, let the prairie close right over;
Better still, when signs are right, sow spelt
Where you last gathered clapping pods
Of beans, or hauled in swales of vetch, or rolled up
The intertangled undergrowth of lush alfalfa.

Too many years of corn, then corn, then corn
Will ruin your fields, and oats will burn them dry;
You see those sunflowers nodding their heads
In sleep? They're lethal: they'll leach your farm away.
But with clever alternations, the land
Regains its energy and rewards you for
Your labor — so long as you're not too shy
To sprinkle it with stinking dung, and redden
Your eyes with clouds of flung wood-ash.

Put stubble-land to fire; it pays off well
When black smoke crackles and orange flames
Run like squalls. No one can say whether
Earth feeds on fire or whether the heat
Purges toxins out of the stagnant damp;
Maybe it opens earth's pores and sucks up nutrients
For seeding-time, or closes them tight against
Hail, freezing rain, and the golden hammers of
Noonday sun.
    The man who goes over his fields
And bangs the clods apart with hoe or harrow
Has angels on his shoulders and they look down
Smiling — so does the farmer who, having ridged the prairie,
Cross-plows, and breaks the furrows down.
            Such men
Are giants of the earth, and they command their fields.

ψ

Wet midsummers, clear, hard winters,
Earth sleeping under level pressing snow:
That's what the farmer likes — That combination,
And, in spring, the fields come alive. After
Sowing-time, firm up the soil
And even out the ridges — that way you can guide
Long snakes of water down your seed-rows
From an upland dam or stream. If the surface
Is crazed with dried mud-biscuits and white grass
Snaps under your boots, open your sluice-gates;
Clear water, in a pulse of liquid crystal,
Rattles down the runnel-stones; fields
Sop it up and your feet slap about
In sudden pools and the slaked earth breathes again.
Sometimes young shoots of corn
Spike upward before their season and, fearing
The weight of early-burgeoning cobs,
You have to graze your flocks to prune them down.
From wetlands, cut a ditch, fill it with
Medium gravel; cover it over:
Square pipe without a wall, it draws trapped water
Away from flooded creek-flats, leaving
Muddy bottom-lands that smoke in the evening sun.

ψ

Watch out for geese and cranes who scrabble
Among the shoots, trampling flat, in a chaos
Of web-marks, everything you've sown;
Lamb's tongue, velvet-leaf, crab-grass — gangs of weeds
And their night-companion, Shade: these continual
Adversaries — for, whoever began it all
Created these things to test our brains
And he is most successful: we worry constantly.

Before the beginning of things no farmers came
To hack out their living in squared plats
Marked off by hedges and boundary stones.
All things were held in common then
And earth put forth her gifts without measure.

Whoever it was, first alchemist of life and death,
He filtered poison for the snake's hollow fang
He also taught the wolves to scavenge, and seas
To toss about. He stole all nectar
From the leaves, outlawed fire and dammed
The river of wine that once flowed everywhere —
And he made us think, experiment, and brood.

Out of our anxious minds, very slowly,
He caused all hand-crafts to begin: wood-plows for corn,
Rock-wedges for finding fire that hides in flint,
And boats, hollowed from alder-trees, whose sailors
Named the stars: Hunter, Wagoner, Big Bear.

ψ

Then came the age of traps and springes:
Hungry men and hounds, leashed together,
Heads forward, combing the forest-brakes
Like shadows; the time of nets, weighted
In dark rivers, and trawling-lines, hauled hissing
Between islands; then carbon-steel, and saws
With blades that screamed and whanged
(Men of the rocks split wood with wedges of stone).
Then all the arts sprang up. Out of crude necessity
Work had created time for the shuttle and loom, time
For the hum of the potter's wheel, study, and singing.

ψ

As the mother of grain taught men to plow
With metal blades, whole groves of acorns
And the so-called Strawberry plant grew thinner,
As if the whispering oaks had banished them.
But soon a shadow leaned over the croplands:
Green rust crept up the stalks like worms,
Eating their life away; empires of tough thistles
With purple flowers and helmets of thorn
Took over. Where once the crop stood tall
In gleaming rows, bugloss and cocklebur reared
Their prickly heads and spread their flat green tongues.

ψ

Times like that
                  you go to war: you hack
And sweat in a surf of weeds,
                              you rig up
Scarecrows and noise-machines,
                                  make mad music
For seed-carrying birds
                        and you attack Shade
By slashing its roots away.
                            If not
You'll gaze with envy as your
                              neighbor's silos
Brim with golden grain,
                      and find yourself
Shaking an oak-tree hard,
                      for a hatful of nuts
To grind up
            for your daily acorn-bread.

ψ

Now to implements and tools which all
Serious farmers need, sowing and harvesting:
First, plows and harrows, their blades and tines
Dirt-free, smooth, sharpened for their work,
Correctly angled with hammer and file and
Like a horse, always ready.
                              For small fields,
Mattocks and hoes, their handles oiled
And seasoned. You know the saying:
Idle hands make nothing but hungry bellies.

A threshing-floor's always level. Flatten it
With a roller, tamp it by hand and cram
The cracks with a mix of clay and lime
To suffocate the weeds and leave no home
For opportunistic pests: the skinny mouse
Anxious to build his granaries underground
And the blind mole mining his endless catacombs.
Toads also feed on your neglect by hiding
In cavities you've missed, and one small team
Of weevils can churn a hill of corn to powder.

And don't forget Field-Marshall Ant.
He's smart: he'll commandeer your grain
As a pensioner's home — for no one but himself.

ψ

A shock of fragrant almond-blossom, should it persist,
Is an excellent sign. If followed by thick
Clumps of nuts, your harvest's as good as in;
Likewise, when the sun's a flaming rag on your neck.
But if our acquaintance, Shade, has been at work
And the ground's obscured with elephant ears of burdock,
You'll have no grain to separate from a chaff
Of frayed skunk-cabbage and strings of fiber.

I've know some farmers who douse their seed
In alkali and tubs of tar-black olive-oil
To ensure their midget beans will swell
And fill their pods so, when they're shelled
And brought to boil over the slenderest flame,
They're quickly soft to the bite.
                                          I've also noticed
Even when you cull them year after patient year
Rejecting runts and throwbacks, the seeds are always
Reverting to their ancestors. You're like a boatman
Climbing a mountain-stream: if you relax your arms
Just once, you're flailing backwards in white water.

ψ

Like sailors, hauling homeward through
Tide-rips and the razor-backed seething pulks
Of oyster-beds, we have to read the stars,
Especially Arcturus, guardian of the Bear,
Also the Young Goats, and the Snake.

                                        From the time
When light and dark are held in a delicate
Equipoise, sow barley whenever you can;
Sow barley right to the edge of winter.

from
POINTS IN A JOURNEY
1966

POINTS IN A JOURNEY

The House in the Bush

It's light, the long egg-tomatoes
Hang still; it's light and my bones feel green.
I bounce on the bed while the pee-wees
Yodel in the gums. There's one

Takes witchetties from our hands, then scoots
To a branch. Today I'll climb my tree
To get that Black Prince, or a fat
Greengrocer, hang recklessly

By a leg. Or go with Dad into
The huge paddock, like yesterday,
Looking for snakes — while the northwind
Pushed back the hay.

Last night the trees were black, and still
And when he slept I slid down
And watched the stars moving;
We were together and alone.

Wake, wake! Sh, better be quiet.
Someone's in the kitchen: Auntie.
She coughs at night. Yesterday
She clicked her needles, and watched me

And yelled *Be Careful*. Her lips are hard.
I'll start from that branch. It's easy.
It's very quiet — except when the train
Whistles. Hey, it's light! *Hey,*

Wake up!

The First Day

I want to get next to my brother.
   Garn, get back, I'm first.
I want to get next to my brother.
Garn!
        I tighten my fist

And smack the face. My brother
   Says 'That's Ronnie Salt, and
What did you hit him for?
   There's warm blood on my hand.

At the River

A day of cloud and the grey Hawkesbury
Winding under the bridge, and four
Kids waist-deep in the slow water
Squinting in the noon's glare.

Laughing, he grabs my legs, and I
Strike out, and move away. He's followed,
Watching; trips me again, and we wrestle
Fiercely, flop about, and break — to brood

Apart. But when he charges and
Dumps me, I swallow mud
And a white madness flares — and I
Clutch him pressing his head

Down on the sand in the thrashed water.
He can't wriggle when I squat
Over his chest, and his eyes roll,
Wide with fear and hate

As I force him down. And I will
Kill you, brother — but for this man with hard
Hands wrenching me off, yelling,
Want to drown him, you young bastard?

A day of cloud and the grey Hawkesbury
Winding under the bridge, and four
Kids waist-deep in the slow water
Squinting in the noon's glare.

Concord

Beneath the hilarity
   Of guns and kites
There's a raw wound won't heal:
In a driven city
   At separate desks, we learn
To make plans and conceal.

Trades

Why are your hands so grease-black, mine
So smooth? Your fat blue book
Shows diagrams of conrods, bolts;
Why does my mind hate
This multiplicity of things,
Their hard outlines?

A Time of Gold

This is a time of dangerous gold:
Gold of the lectern and the cold
Burnished capitals of the bible.
Slow-gold of the incredible
Summer across the quiet land.
Sea-gold: two bodies in the sand,
Blind with the gold searing
In the blood — clasping, flaring
Of gold within gold.
                    More dangerous still,
More dangerous than the metal of the will,
The gold of knowledge. I have a serious
Hurt look, a cherrywood pipe, various
Gimmicks to disarm. My quick tongue
Swims — I think — in gold. I sing
To please myself, and am successful.
I'm splenetic with a hesitant fool
At first handshake. I talk with
Friends on metaphysics, myth,
And sometimes listen, till the dawn
Light spreads, when wilder thoughts will spawn
Thickly. The world seethes. And my mind
Races, and is almost blind.

Worlds

I think it strange that two who keep
The same cluttered room, who breathe, and sleep
So near — two who had come
So closely from a single womb —
Should guard such heavy silences.

Your morning world of black distances
Where the faint light breeds and a lone tram
Rocks down the hill, is not my home.
Two hours I toss while the light jells
To a new day. Your body-smells
Float, your curious presence lingers.
I rise and eat; with nervous fingers
Pack my texts. My morning world
Is grey-suited men curled
Behind their papers, hard light, schoolboys
Fooling about on trams. In the noise,
Striving to concentrate, to
Make it cohere, I think of you
Pulling controls, watching blue steel
Curl from the lathe, checking the angle
Of a drill.   Today we have a class
On Pope. Tomorrow, Milton. My case
Brims with knowledge, yet I am dumb
At table: the simple words won't come.

Our skill's evasion. Often
At weekends when we are just young men
Dressed out for tennis, or reading, we come
Upon each other in a quiet room
Unexpectedly, and then we look
Uneasy, ashamed — and almost speak.

Battersea: Just before Dark

Two photographs pinned on my wall
Look down now as I write:
Your children caught in a quizzical
Pose, and you — all strangely still;

The other, a garden — a tree
And a paling fence, the stage
In this. On the left, a family —
Three generations indolently

Sprawl on the lawn, or stand
Awkward. Who are these images
Whose blood throbs in my moving hand,
Whose nerves sing in my mind?

The ambiguity remains
Of far and near. Surely the last child
Whom I haven't held, retains
Familiar mouldings in her bones.

Two pigeons at my window fly
Out to darkness. And you look down
Smiling, so strange, a million grey
Waves, and all these deaths away.

AUTUMN AFTERNOON, WITH BIRDS

It's an afternoon of birds in a low sky:
Starlings and blackbirds and indifferent pigeons
Drift past the grey square of my window
To flitter in trees or strut on the roof-tops.
The year's going down, the last warmth seeps away,
And those who amble in the flat parklands
Inhale the skeleton-promise of the trees —
And as these dark bodies dip, or thrust by,
I think of birds in another country:
The straight crane steering himself leisurely
Over the swamp at sundown; the spry wagtail
Hopping from stone to bough to stone. I yield
No place to myth-birds; dream of flesh and feathers:
The mollyhawk and the scrawny gull, swinging
To leeward in a pure white curve, watching.
The concealed bell-bird — and the terse wedge-tail
Riding with still wings on the wind-rivers —

And once we watched the blue teal, winding
Their circle down a wide valley
Learning the land's shape for the spring
Before they turned out northward to the sun.

Here they wade and fall in the smoky air
Over the stained, repetitive houses
That stretch in tight reefs, unendingly —
Out to Clapham, Fulham, Lavender Hill;
Mostly indifferent pigeons. Still, a man
Is not like that. Look with what skill
That one kicks off the ledge, flies out
And up to the roof-top; lives in his body,
Does not strive.

A MILD JUNE DAY

I have been grave all afternoon;
Full of responsibility, heavy
With sense of failure; riffled an hour
Through manuscripts, jotted and scowled

Achieving nothing. I forget
What drew me to the window
Where I stood, half-seeing fragments
Of sky, the sooted backs of tenements.

Then suddenly you laughed, and I
With you when you had told the phrase.
At which 'Responsibility' seemed only
A pious lie, 'duty'
A name for fear.
Perhaps our only measure
If we reflect, is unexpected pleasure.

A dry bird flicked across the roof,
And I was grave again, thinking,
If we should lose that gift —
Afraid to amuse,
Forced in the intricacies of pride to choose
Each word, each act —
It would be best to go:
It would be best to turn, and quickly go.

REFUSING SONG

When maybe a sparrow clicked his nail
On the dry slate, and a barrowman called
Something somewhere below maybe;
So many rhythms in the air,
But one especially that ran
Over and over drowsily
As the sun dropped from the world's edge,
This is the nearest warmth that we can know.

And maybe slept as the dark came.
There was a train that grumbled, miles below.
I was too vigilant, too tense,
Unsure of everything except
The rhythm that ran in my brain
Over and over drowsily
Because this contentment cannot last
Though it's the only warmth that we can know.

DETAIL OF AN ESTRANGEMENT

Each night there's been a queer complaint in the door;
Like a branch that squeaks in a light wind, or
A trapped insect pressing to get loose.
We've listened, tapped, watched close
For an answer — found nothing. *Perhaps a knot*
Stretching in the young wood, or some trick of the heat
Has it creak that way. . .
And then we've slept, forgotten.
                                              Once more, day
Whitens the room, and it squeals again, like a dry
Gimlet turning. Nearing six;
The throats of a dozen cocks
Rending the quiet as I wait and dream
Lazy images while the first flies come —
Sheet over nose, thinking a little of death.
                                                         And she
Turns, and squints out of a narrowed eye,
Peers about with subdued hostility;

And I ask myself *'is there a germ that squats*
Cunning at the heart of luck; which waits,
Then kills?' There was no quarrel, nor lapse of tact;
The day turned round and we were strangers in it.
And now we wait in silence
For some inexplicable revenge.
Turning away from that, last night we hunted
Perhaps for an insect trapped in the wood,
Pretending, diffidently joking;
But today we must admit there's a thing
Newly dead, and not be over courteous with its burial,
Knowing it must be quick or it will
Breed with the slow logic of decay —
Whether we strike out, or yell, or say
Nothing. Sometimes the world sickens with its realities:
Mussed hair, this noise in the wood, eyes
Clenched in feigned sleep. And I can mend. Or can break! Or
Rise bewildered, paste in my mouth, a liar
By defection,
                          to clack pebbles
Along the beach, smoke and forget — as well as
One might after such crime — looking for some
Huge lesson in this. Or someone to blame.

TWO SPANISH PIECES

Morning Music
Something is singing in the woman
Who knocks with her broom on the hard flags;
An old Ibicenko tune I'd say
For it leaps and quivers in a strange
Ambiguous mode. I know the face: she's a tooth
In each mouth corner, blackness between.
Her hand cupped on the broom-end, she'll talk
Out of that gap for a neat half-hour
Her round belly shaking as she guffaws.
But now the voice fights in her throat
And breaks free in a furred glissando,
And on the bed's edge
Watching day ripen, I'm glad of it
As it rings in the hall, climbs the stairwell:
A little thread of contentment — while the fascist guard
Patrols in the public square, his holsters shining.

Late Summer
The man who woke me with his tuneless whistle,
Outside my window in the thinning
Dawn, has quick fingers to get the almonds
And the cracked husks gape in mounds
That build at his feet. The women spread figs. Soon
They'll cut and press each sticky one
To a next, making mound-of-Venus-shape fruits
For the sun, to be piled on white plates,
Heavy with overdrinking, dry
With a puckered blue-brown satiety.

And that's the problem: last year he snipped back
Each gnarled, empty vinestock
To a winter outline; and yesterday we broke
Full grapes in our mouths. The pulp
Ran sweet down our throats, while around
The left ones hung in their green light —

When to let flourish, when to pare?

He whistles now, and cracks the shells. Right
Near, long cornleaves clash in a moistening wind.

SLEEPLESS IN FLORENCE

Because of a pain that erupted, and the heat.
Round three a cat yowled somewhere below.
I dozed a little, woke to a mewl of cats
And French voices that ricocheted in the empty lanes.
I made for the window, pressing my belly,
Intending something but with no clear plan —
As a swinging load of water smacked the cobbles.
There was a startled *Que c'est moche!* Then silence,
And the French dispersed. But the cats slowly
Regained their ground. I watched them striding,
Velvet-padded, then more bold in the shadows.
Large and quick, they'd tear the pelt from any dog
Who came by, sniffing ingenuously. A woman
With bleak eyes, hair knotted with sleep, staring
From the opposite window, upturned her basin,
Grinned at me, then closed the shutters.
                                            I leant, to study
How they'd melt and re-appear, crying like a man
Wounded beyond his understanding, or
With a quick snarl snatching the next one's crust.

We had three rolls, baked hard by August heat
Which I weighed in my palm, as I squinted down.
The shutter made such an angle to the wall
I'd crack my wrist-bone if I hurled it. I waited.
At length a white one came, paused on the flags,
Cried up the strairwell to god knows whom.
I measured the angle, still couldn't throw.
The roll was like a light hard ball in my hand
And I wanted him to climb another foot; but he stayed
Poised in the mauve light, just out of range.

CONTRARIES: DECEMBER

Something denser perhaps. Than bits of snow
Balanced on the wind, lighting and melting
Against old timber in a factory yard.
A thing more rich, and something solider
Than the empty grey light of these three rooms
Where my footsteps echo and stop. I pluck
A dry chord from the guitar, set it down.
A square truck rattles past, whirling the snow.
Someone real, an animal, a woman
Humming into the fire, sharing the cold.
★

Broken toys in the hallway, thick
Yellow lamplight, and basement smells of stew.
We plunge from early dark into intense
Pools of yellow light; we, millions.
The stairs fall back slowly.   All families
Have a cabbage-smell; nonetheless, tired of my own
Boundaries, I think of others, imagine voices
Of other children. These things I want,
And I reject my want, preferring
Long nights where the phone squats quietly.
★

I know enough to say that snow is wrong —
As it packs the angles of walls, and spreads
Touching all forms with ignominy:
Strange stuff that, singly, can't resist the heat
Of a cupped hand, yet builds, and heavy,
And trodden has a look of quiet permanence.
Other things — still props for a sluggish mind —
As rock, or the colour green — not posing
As beyond, will do perhaps. But snow's
A sign for purity, and always wrong.

★

That sharp-boned miser, hugging his candle-flame,
Peaked and costive — a horrible man!
In a wide room with light and tinsel
We ignore details: the deep
Bewilderment of children, the small hand
That selects and clutches. Even our hates
Have lost their edge. Refill your whisky.
This child has a clear beauty. Jiggle
His bright unnecessary toy.
                                          A man
Half-understood, his cold thought out of season

★

These hanging cards: outback scenes, holly,
St. Francis ringed with geometric birds —
A few scratched words to ease astringent
Silences. Tokens, I thought. Except
That yesterday in one or two I found
Something most shy and tentative — and I stood
Perplexed with my ingratitude, as the thin
Flakes, now tenuous but individual,
Fell straight, and with disappointing quickness
Fused with the general moisture on the ground.

★

A child attacks me with a water-gun,
Trips, gashes his eye. I like the way
He checks his weeping while the frightened blood
Stains his hand. The house is heavy with smells
Of sickness. The woman cries out to the snow.
Her husband brings her blankets as I comfort
The boy, who suddenly grows calm,
And grins. The day steadies.
This year I'll try to praise what's warm:
What's suffering, ambiguous, uncertain.

THE WATER MAN

A Narrative for Voices

1976

performed on the BBC, February 1983
& Australian National Radio, March 1983

CHARACTERS
(in order of appearance)

Announcer

Evert Everstrud

Roxanne, Rusty's wife

Rusty Everstrud, *elder son of Evert*

Jason Everstrud, *younger son of Evert*

Lucy, *Jason's wife*

Roger Everstrud, *Jason's and Lucy's son, aged six*

First Foreman

Second Foreman

The setting is rural Minnesota

ANNOUNCER

Not like a ticker tape that clicks out minutes in
Rigid rows. Not like the metal wheel that squats
On your wrist, insisting, *Now, now, now.*
For this man, time is a pool of living images in which
He swims, un-touching, wherever he might choose.
He can stretch the years, or squeeze them to a tiny bauble.
Two little words contain an age of lust unsatisfied;
Thirty years is the flick of a blackbird's wing.

However a man stains the pool when living,
When he's left his body,
Nothing can wash away that stain.

Here's Everstrud, who lost himself in water, while
His two sons, Rusty and Jason
Are breathing, now, as you listen to these words.

Low humming sound

EVERSTRUD

This house always my home, I split the wind
And send it fizzing like cold surfwater
Around the pig-barn and the milking-shed
And ride with it in bubbles of light.
Or, in October, when the back-lit clouds hang still,
Fly up and wait beside the screech owl,
The moon shuttering in his yellow eye.
Those nights I like the way the light slides
Over the smooth lawn, always trimmed,
Remembering me, old Everstrud, who sliced
His hand on the bailer: fat blood-drops
Dappled the grass as he sprinted to the kitchen;
And Rusty who took that painted slut for wife —
All in white on the summer lawn, smooth-shaven:
Fifty years.
            They think I'm still down there
Dissolving in my bones, but I've swum up
Through the black lakewater. Swum home. There's a sign
NO TRESPASSING. But I trespass all the time.

You've seen those long festoons of kelp
In troubled water — the waves lifting
And thrashing them against black rocks:
Their filaments and shattered cells
Go out, and out, invisible atoms
Romping with the tides. The sea is everything it holds:
Flotsam, quick bodies; steaming whales
Anemones and bones. There everything's at home.
And so I ride with every wind that
Kicks up from my long-fallowing wheatfields.

Soon they'll come clanking down the road
With iron jaws — to flatten my barn
And set down painted bungalows. But I will stay
As the wind will stay — and sometimes in the silence
When a raised spoon hesitates
At the doorway of your mouth, when at dawn
A fir-branch rubs the window rapidly
Like a large cat that no one ever finds,
I shall breathe among you and feel
Your skins tighten as the owl winks

> High in the hayloft, and somewhere a drunken tide
> Pounds the rock platforms and out of its belly breeds
> New strings of bladderwrack that lick the continents —
> Where I can no longer touch my wounded hand.

Music. Slow, deep cello.

EVERSTRUD
Roxy...

ROXANNE
What is it, old man, you feelin' hungry again?
You already ate five ribs and a plate of potatoes.

EVERSTRUD
I know you're fixin' to marry him . . .

ROXANNE
That's right. Soon as he can make it home.

EVERSTRUD
That's fine, it's just that...

ROXANNE
Just what?

EVERSTRUD
It's just that I was hankerin to take you rowin.
Just friendly like. The moon's full up,
It's helluva pretty out there.

ROXANNE
I want you to tell me why you hate him.

EVERSTRUD
Well...it's not. . .

ROXANNE
Look — he's nowhere in the house. You can tell me.
I don't go blabbin to Rusty about everythin.
I just want to know, that's all. Sometimes when I see
You two hunched together — the silence and the watchin —
It puts a taste of metal in my mouth.
He won't say nothin. Is it so terrible
You can't even think about it?

EVERSTRUD
Well, I never told no one this —
But I been thinkin about it — must be twenty years.
(pause)
I would have fathered him like I fathered Jason, but . . .

ROXANNE
But?

EVERSTRUD

Well. . . I was kinda tricked into it all —
The matherin, I mean. By god, Roxy,
I was itchy then — and too crazy-young
To marry. But Alice's folks and my old man
Dressed me up for the preacher
And we signed the book and they shut it.
Then they all gathered
Round me, real close, and told me:
STOP ITCHIN AND START WORKIN — and I did.
> *(pause)*

I'm sixty-three, and the itchin's never stopped.
> *(they laugh)*

EVERSTRUD *(quietly)*

Ah, Roxy. . . let's row across to the other side. . .

ROXANNE

You ever get the feelin that this place
Is under the sea — the currents pourin over us
Every which way? But tonight it's like an animal
Waitin for somethin to move out there in the grass.
Listen, you can hear the whole world breathin.

EVERSTRUD

We could find some of them big smooth stones —
Some of them moon-rocks — for Jason's boys.

ROXANNE

She's up there all alone, old man.
I heard the bed complainin as she turned.

EVERSTRUD

She's sleepin.

ROXANNE

Old man, you've got a wife upstairs whose bones
Are stickin out all over and you take no mind of her
Two minutes in any day.

EVERSTRUD

Look at that light jumpin on the water!

ROXANNE

Sit, down, old man — it's late.

EVERSTRUD

Ah, Roxy. . . .

ROXANNE

The name's Roxanne. I'm marryin your son.
You'll have to get your moon-rocks by yourself!

Music.

RUSTY

Roxy. . .

ROXANNE

What? Oh, Rusty. How long you been there?

RUSTY

Few minutes. Watchin you gawp through the window.
I never seen you stand like that, just gawpin.
What you up to? You got somethin on your mind?

ROXANNE

Must be the time of year. Your Dad again.
I been thinkin about him. He never goes away.
And I been wonderin what's up at Jason's place.
I swear there's nothin moved since Monday —
The tractor's stuck there by the corn-rick,
The pick-up's in pieces all over the yard,
And Lucy's car just sits. Three whole days.

RUSTY

Yeah, I heard him too — when the mower quit.
I called on Jason to get some tools.
Jason was gone and Lucy'd shut herself
On the dark side of the house,
The room the three boys used to sleep in.
I tried the door. Locked from the inside.
It was quiet down there. Too quiet.

ROXANNE

Feedin on memories, feedin on sorrow.
She won't eat anythin Jason cooks for her.
She's nothin but bones, her big eyes
Frighten me. Rusty, she's got to get movin.
One time, chores took most of her day, now Jason
Does most everythin.

(pause)

I'm feelin strange this mornin.
Time of year when things come back.
Few minutes ago your Dad was right here
At the table, smell of liquor on his breath
And his voice husky. Wantin to take me rowin.
Always the same. I kicked him out,
But you never know which way he's comin.

RUSTY
He can happen out of a stone. One time
He jumped at me from behind a tree
And caught me with a handful of tobacco —
And if he saw me tryin to hide
A nudie magazine under my shirt he'd come down
Like a wheat bag fallin on my chest.
ROXANNE
You would have killed him so I never told you.
The month before we married
He called me a slut — no, not to my face.
I heard him all the same. One of those days
When the beer was foamin fast from the keg
Back of the chicken-shed. He was jokin with 'the boys'.
I heard him say it and I heard *them* whinnyin
At my expense — and I could see
Their yellow lips, and hear their big boots stompin —
So I ran from the house and went straight up to him.
Two inches from his eye I said: *You called me somethin?*
Now, I reckon you're old enough to know
The difference — or maybe you're so past it
You can't even tell a woman from your hand.

That stopped him — stopped them laughin too,
Right in their scrawny throats. They looked down at their boots
And jammed their beer-cups back into their mouths
And they never bothered me again.

But from that time on he hated me, and wanted me.
RUSTY
And any woman with hot blood in her.
ROXANNE
Ah, let's forget all that, it's gone down the wind.
It's over.
RUSTY
Just as the mower stopped a wind slammed
Outa the south and flicked a bird at my head —
I watched it go like a black bullet over the roof,
And then I heard him: *You must sell my house.*

No tellin where it came from. And then
The wind banged round the other way

And I heard him somewhere back of the barn:
You must never sell my house.
                                             Old bastard.
You never know which way his mind is blowin.
But, I tell you, more than anythin I'd like to kill him
For good. Right now. (yelling) *Stay still
Hog-face, so I can finally kill you!*

ROXANNE.

Rusty, we can forget about him.
We have to think about the livin.
What's up at Jason's place? Nothin's movin
Down there. They should be harvestin.

Sound of wind, fairly faint.

LUCY

The tractor's shot, admit it. You spend your time
Your head stuck in a useless engine.

JASON

Last year the crop gave almost nothin, Lucy,
And you know the bank won't back us now
For anythin. I have to fix this up as best I can
And bring the harvest in.

LUCY

Useless.

JASON

It isn't useless, but it's difficult. Everythin's worn.
But with a little time. . .

LUCY

Time, time, time. What do you know about time?
It wasn't you who carried them..

JASON

I know, Lucy. You told me. . .

LUCY

No — it wasn't you who carried them three years.
It wasn't your body they lived in all that time.
Three years, then seven more. Then nothin.
Time, time — and what did you do? Up, down,
Plow, plow, seven years, what do you do
With nothin in your head, Jason? Nothin,
And a broken engine — oh, yes,
Fine farm we have here, full of nothin but wind.
(*goes*)

EVERSTRUD (V.O.)
What's a matter, son? Bad season?
JASON (*as if talking to himself*)
I'm sick of walkin backwards — that's what's the matter.
Every day, my mouth full of stones, and nothin works
And the bank's gone dry on me. On this place
I'm carryin everythin — her and me, and the memories
And the guilt and. . . everythin — and now you again.
Shut up. Get the hell outa my mind
EVERSTRUD
Why don't you do it, son?
JASON
Do what?
EVERSTRUD
You know what, you been thinkin about it. Weeks
JASON
Shut up. Get back in the wind where you belong.
EVERSTRUD
It's easy, Jason. Real easy. Then you're free.
You can float any direction, night or day.
No wives, or banks, or clocks to bother you.
Think about it, son.
JASON
Look. I got a job to do. Clear out,
And leave me alone.

Sound of wind.

LUCY (*off to one side*)
It wasn't him who carried them.
It wasn't his body they lived in.
(pause)
Tommy was quick as a bird in a stubble-field.
He hid all Roger's clothes in the crook of a tree.
Roger's eyes were like the sea; after a sleep
He smelt like bread. And last came Nick
His foot twisted. He talked to himself
All night and hugged the dark.
(pause)
Wind, then nothing on the water.

Roar of a car engine. Sound of Jason running)

JASON (yelling)
Come back here, you old madman. The tie rod's loose.
Bring them back!

LUCY
What's happenin, Jason?

JASON
The old man's taken the boys for a ride.
Christ, why can't he come and ask?

LUCY
All, three of them? Just when I needed them
For chores! Didn't I tell you, Jason
Never leave the keys in the ignition!
Never leave the keys when there are kids around.

JASON
I never *left* them. I was workin on it.
I was in the tool-shed huntin for a pin
To hold the tie-rod. With the generator whinin
I never heard him.

LUCY
You mean the steerin's loose! We got to stop him!

ROGER (V.O)
Gramps smelled like whisky, Gramps showed me how to drive.
Stuck me between his legs and put his hands
Right over mine. His fingers looked like lizards
And we were flyin'

JASON (at the 'phone)
Charlie? Jason Everstrud. Emergency, Charlie.
The old man's taken the kids again. He's headin toward
The lake down 93. Can you head him off?
The tie-rod's loose. My pick-up's out of gas,
And there's no one home at Rusty's.
The old bastard's drivin like a madman! *(pause)*
You gotta catch him, Charlie!

ROGER (V.O.)
Gramps was laughin in the wind, and so were we!

JASON
Oh, no, he's taken the switchback road!
Look at the dust, he's almost flyin!
The police car's not chasin him,
It's ahead of him — two miles *ahead* of him.

ROGER
Gramps was laughin. Our hands told the Chevy
Go there, over the bridge. . .
LUCY
Don't just squat there, Jason. Do somethin.
JASON
There's nothin . . . Charlie's tryin . . .
ROGER (V.O)
Gramps was laughin. Our hands told the Chevy
Go there, over the bridge,
But it jumped the other way. Gramps
Held me in his knees, and up we flew.
EVERSTRUD
I locked my knees on Roger as the nose
Lifted, everythin poured into my ears.
I heard the motor turnin for a second after
We dove. Ah, Jesus it was cold down there.

Silence, then the sound of winching machinery.

FIRST FOREMAN
It's too far I tell you. Why didn't you bring
Your other cable? This one's comin to pieces.
And it's too short anyway. You got a longer cable?
SECOND FOREMAN
No. But even with that we'd never make it.
It's only guessin. You need a special grapplin. . .
FIRST FOREMAN
Look, I know those people. We gotta try.
SECOND FOREMAN
We're tryin! Who was it?
FIRST FOREMAN
Everstrud.
SECOND FOREMAN
Not Jason!
FIRST FOREMAN
No — his old man. He always said
Nothin could kill him. He got that wrong.
It was him, and Jason's boys.
SECOND FOREMAN
All three of them?

FIRST FOREMAN
Yeah, all three. Hell, I can see bubbles down there.
Look! They could still be breathin.
You got a diver on your team?
SECOND FOREMAN
There's no diver for a hundred miles.
FIRST FOREMAN
Look, they're still alive down there.
We've gotta find some way.
SECOND FOREMAN
It's down a hundred feet. This cable's seventy,
There isn't time.

Winching sound fading to silence

LUCY *(V.O.)*
Wind and nothing on the water.
(Pause, quiet music)
RUSTY
He whipped me once just like you'd whip a dog —
For stealin a few old apples the birds
Had got to first, and told me I'm no good
For anythin — told me I'd spend my life
Sloppin pigswill in a ditch. I could feel
He hated my roots. So I shut him out,
And never spoke to him unless he spoke.
Later, I made a promise to myself:
I'd keep the whole thing cut, exactly right
Each Sunday — and he'd see I got it
Better than he could, ever — and feel
The hate that rose up my arms like steam.
Every Sunday.
(pause, then strongly)
And I will keep you shuntin about in hell
Till all the winds go dead and the earth
Turns over on its back, and everythin's
Black ice again — black ice, and stone.
ROXANNE
Forget about him now, forget the lawn.
You've kept it for him all these years.
Let the whole place crack, and rot into the ground.
Leave go of him. Let's think about the livin.

RUSTY

You don't understand. I promised.

ROXANNE

Promised yourself — and you can
Break it. Rusty, it's time to leave go.

(music pause)

ROXANNE

Where is she, Jason?

JASON

I don't know, she ran out, headin
Toward the lake again. She doesn't care.
Doesn't want me, doesn't want anyone..

ROXANNE

Did you try talkin?

JASON

Roxanne, I been tryin for years. Told her and told her.
Told her, Lucy, we'll never make them swim up out of it,
Gently as I could, *we have to try,*
We have our neighbors and our friends,
And all this good land around us, and
We have ourselves — told her, *Lucy, we have to live right now.*
(pause)
The few words she spat at me were like cold nails
Knocked into my skull. When she ran out last time
I began to think, if the house will always be
Without their voices, if all that remains
Is emptiness and sorrow, it'd be best
To give my body to the corn.
(pause)

ROXANNE

So you stopped tryin?

JASON

Yeah, after so many times and so much
Nothin, I went for a walk up the hill with
The three firs. I could smell my own death
In my nostrils. Hers too. One flesh, the preacher says.
I needed time.
(pause)

ROXANNE

Keep talkin.

JASON

I sat there hours, hidden in the trees, my mind
Teeterin: *No. Yes* — then a final *No.* Then I began figurin
Figurin how. I could see his old house, a mile away,
Where Rusty still mows the lawn — why so perfect
I never knew — but I had troubles of my own.
I sat there, listenin to my heartbeat and the wind.

ROXANNE

I noticed you gone a long time, and . . .

JASON

There was a blue jay, Roxy — this sounds crazy, I know —
There was a blue jay — and somethin about his clumsy leapin
Pulled me out. I looked at myself, squattin there,
Half-hungerin for the ground, and there *it* was
Jippin about, half off-balance and, you know,
He seemed to be laughin at me — and, finally,
He jumped out into the blue, and I thought: *Hell,*
I'm thirty-eight, why should I fill my mouth
With clay? Perhaps, I'm not too smart,
But there's a good life flowin in me.
Yes, maybe we can put some new life on the place —
Some orphaned kids who need a home,
And a long-locked room in my head
Burst open and I heard the old goat and
The three boys chuckle, down there in the water
And I threw a rock clear down to the creek,
And laughed into the space where the blue jay'd
Disappeared. And I had chosen.

ROXANNE

I saw you hurryin down the road . . .

JASON

I walked in and found her dozin
In the boy's room on the cold side of the house.
She's always in that room, and I said to her,
Very quiet, *Lucy, I been thinkin — up there*
Among the firs. Like you, I've been full of grievin
And I couldn't see how to go on — now I know we can.
If only. . . We're still young, Lucy —
Perhaps we can help some kids — give them a home —
You know, some kids, unluckier —
                                       I'd been talkin
To the hills and lakes in the picture

Above her head, not wantin to touch
Her body with my eyes, not seein
The horror that must've been spreadin
Over her face. She got up from the bed.
It was like a vase shatterin in your hand.
LUCY (V.O)
You already killed three sons and lost a father,
And you talk of *more* life on this place!
More life to turn to nothin on the water.
Did someone cut your heart out?
Did someone cut your heart out before you were born?
JASON *(quietly)*
Then she ran out to join the wind again, and I knew
There was no way I could follow where she was goin.
LUCY
Wind and nothing on the water
(pause)
RUSTY
I know you're watchin me. Well, look,
Till you're tired of lookin. You never got it
Smooth as that. Exactly an hour
And the edges trimmed and the kitchen
Swabbed clean where the hobos holed up
Last winter. I'm sellin this wreck you call
Your house, and I'm sellin you with it. I'm not listenin
To anythin you say. You never stuck it out.
I did. Sixteen years, and never missed. I'm gonna
Last you out — and you can keep on watchin'.
(pause)
JASON
Ran out to join the wind again. Three days.
And I couldn't follow. When she came back
Her mind was gone, though her body kept
Walkin around. Three months, not listenin
To anythin. You saw how it was — as if
She was honein herself down for dyin. Screamed
At the nurses when they came, ran for a knife.
(pause)
At the last she was only bones, and an old nightie.

And I had chosen.

EVERSTRUD (V.O.)
How many years have I been watchin
Among these spills of wind and water,
Not gettin born again, and never dyin?
(pause)

JASON
I go over it always at the edge of sleep.
These two sons who climb on my back each night, this
Quick-eyed daughter whose parents died for her
Somewhere out there where strange tides flow —
Two sons and a daughter, not of my blood but close
As blood might be — this wife who took my sorrow
And warmed it to a sweet accepting
That almost heals — this new life in my house
And the long fields rising.
                              Last night
The hammer of hail — by noon, the air
So still it seemed a bowl of amethyst, and tall fire.
And when they ask me: 'What turned you away
From broodin on so much loss?' I tell them,
A blue jay, up there in the firs.
(pause)
Sometimes I'm troubled by a dream — the four of them
Locked in, slowly turning to weeds and mud-slime
But I have learned this, to set against
That kind of dreamin: Love is a thing
We choose in solitude, then find as best we can.
And once we find it, like pebble-rings in a pool,
It wants to go out from us. We cannot hold it,
We cannot shape it on our own.

And I have learned another thing that
Rides beside me on the tractor when I turn
At the field's end, and my house is only a pill-box
Shadowed by trees no larger than an eye-lash:
I have learned that when death comes in its
Proper time, it is a gift that
No one may unwrap for us. That is our own,
Not looked for, not denied, and never shared.

(Music)

EVERSTRUD (V.O)
How many years have I been riding
Like a brainless witch about these fields and barns:
A citizen of cracks and dusty darkness.
These cornleaves flying out from Jason's combine
Mean nothin to me, and I am bored
With the speech of owls and badgers.

I watch you all, drowning yourselves in time,
Coupling and dividing, clamped
To the smokey fever of your bones.
        Rusty,
Sleep easy, now, and warm yourself
Against your wife, like a man by a winter stove,
Sleep easy, and keep you promises,
I'm waiting for you.
       And you, Jason
Turn and turn through your slow days:
Dry sticks, and lilac bloom, and rain — while I
Float off to the edge of things trying to
Pass the time but only returning
To this house always my home:
A water man who cannot sleep in water;
A man of wind who scans you all
With eyes of wind, and hungers for his body.

Silence. Then wind, very faint, then music.

PORTRAITS, MASKS
&
MONOLOGUES

PORTRAITS

UNCLE JACK

A thimbleful of the hard stuff
And he was away.
One day he bought a spanking suit
And said, *I'm pissing off to Sydney.*
Returned in a month on the back
Of a clapped out ute
Sporting greasy dungarees, slouch hat
And a mauve wind-cheater
Full of burns and tomato stains.
He gave the suit to a Desert Rat
Fresh from Tobruk on a wharf
Oh, you know,
Somewhere East of Woolloomoolo.

He loved all things
That sprouted from the ground.
His fingers, hard
As the back of a lizard
Touched bulbs and seedlings
The way a man might touch a woman,
And up they sprang —
Colors all around.

And late at night
He'd touch the old piano
Fingers roving along
The delicious notes, finding arpeggio
And chord to suit the color of the breeze:
A kind of song,
Half-major and half-minor —
Hairless head
Nodding over the keys.

As a kid I relished his stories.
Mostly bull, they had the truth
Of legends: the lecherous
Twelve-fingered aristocrat;
The long-limbed hero of his youth
Who pulled three locomotives with his teeth;

The woman who lived in a slum tree-house
And spoke the dialects of Bird and Cat.
Just as we all were getting used
To him, at eighty-six
He pitched head first
Into a dahlia-patch
And flatly refused
To come inside for tea.

When he heard Beethoven his face
Would flush, and when he hummed
The major themes
The notes were all in place.
Sundays his breath was awful.
Last time I walked him to the tram
He said, *I'm*
No good at all.
A scratchy voice, full
Of seawind and the tang
Of plums.
Nonsense, I said
We love you, take it easy.
He half-fell into the tram.

He hungered for wide rivers, the splash
Of a trout, not caught
On his line, but
Leaping free, the flash
Of wild rosellas.
He fought
Too many wars:
One real, wherein
They broke his bones.

And I who could never garden
Worth a damn, measure out
In this leafless room
Ten thimblefuls and another ten
And drink to the music in
His pickled soul — who taught
So many things
To find their brief, unrepeatable bloom.

TWO WOMEN

I'm leaving now, and then packed up his bag
And called a friend to drive him far away.
*You must have known there's someone else — why drag
The whole thing on and on? What more to say?*
Then the doorway went black and the night reeled
And rode into the house like a smoky sea.
She sat an hour, rock-still, then rose and peeled
An apple, left it there to brown, made tea.
Oh there was nothing evil in his going:
He was correct and just in his demands.
But she could just as well prevent the undoing
Of twenty years as kill her trembling hands.
She who had stood by, twenty years beside,
Now stared at night, empty and terrified.

But this one had resources: *I'll prepare
Cherry-stone clams on mounds of fettucini.*
It was his birthday, after all. Why spare
Expense? *And candles, Brie, and Boccherini.*
The meal was perfect — even the small kisses
She'd planned between the first and second course.
And then, at nine, the bell. She rose. *This is
The lawyer, dear. I'm filing for divorce.*
He hardly flinched. *Then one more cup,* he said.
Please, I insist you try this marvelous blend.
He thought of strychnine, poured cognac instead.
In curlicues of smoke they wrote their end.
The lawyer gone, the husband turned on his heel
And thanked her for the *really excellent meal*

A MAN DEAD

A man is dead, one whom we almost knew.
They have laid his body on a table
Embalmed the face, surrounded him with flowers;
And now this image of a living man —
This cold image — waits for the shined box;
Waits for night and the incurious worm.

Tibetan mourners hack their newly dead
Into small pieces for the mouths of birds
Claiming the stiff body's a profanation
Without the informing soul. They hack; and weep —
Remembering the hand that gripped the rice-bowl,
Struck out in rage, or guided the gay kite.

They scatter the redundant flesh on rocks
Beneath the harsh cries of the mountain birds;
Return then to the warm stink of the village
Accepting death as the winter of the body,
Accepting too, the gaiety that breaks out
Despite the hungry birds that hover and fall.

This man went in the flat city whose rites
Are solemn and absurd. I mind his ways:
One called him over-friendly — one, remote;
Another, kind. One hated his sullen rage.
Two things recur though, unarguably lucid:
He was a man once and we almost knew him —

And the short cry that chilled us at the bone.

COLONEL CHEESEMAN'S COMMENCEMENT PARTY
1
A day of pine-smells and early crickets.

In the windless noon I watched a shadow fall
Down the face of Cheeseman's wife and down
Her body while we hunted mushrooms in a field.
At first I thought: *a cloud,*
But the autumn sky was rolling clear. Next day
At the end of surgery
A blood-clot thickened in her leg, rose to her lung
And strangled her.
                              Cheeseman
Patrolled these corridors, days, like a wooden man,
Cursing the walls, then standing
Still as water in a well. Once, at 3 a.m.
He phoned the President,
Cut through the Pentagon's electronic shield:
This is Colonel Cheeseman, Mr. President.
Those bastards at the Mayo killed my wife.
The President murmured drowsy regrets, turned over,
One more nail in his mind.

Exactly a twelvemonth later, unbalanced by grief
And whisky, Cheeseman toppled, spiking
His temple on a fender, and he is ashes
In a bottle somewhere now.
His wide bum used to warm this chair I've sat on
Fifteen years, slowly changing
His musty office to a private must
That's all my own: books and papers,
This heady trade that, with the fume of lilacs
And the colored frisbees planing,
Today seems out of tune, out of time.

I often think of Cheeseman — feckless fellow
Full of gas and appalling jokes.
He'd clubbed it in the army twenty years,
Grafted to an overstuffed chair,
Clutching the same bourbon
Ten thousand times. Garrulous, unlovable
And gross, he had in him some kind of heat —
Our kind of heat, and a gentleness with cats.

2

Bits of us everywhere:
Old boxes in Australia,
Cards from Chicago, green spoons
In a London attic.
The children shuttle between us
And we are several, with pieces
Of a single name, each one of us
Just one more than Cheeseman.

Because I need some rooted thing
I have set down twenty fruit-trees.
I like the body-smell
Of windfalls rotting in the fall,
Anything dense, and living:
This apple you tossed me
Through the morning light — how it shone
When I rubbed it along my sleeve!

And I thought of Jan Vermeer, the stillness.

3

The chuttering of a motor-mower
Floats through my window, Cheeseman's window.
They're trimming lawns, breaking out chairs in rows.
Soon we'll put on black and call this day
Commencement Day.   Cheeseman's out of it,
Once again. No more
Bad jokes in the corridor.

Something of his heat clings to my chair.

THE ECSTASY OF KARMSTAD KARLESON

Under roof-trees where bantams listen, like snow-
light gliding everywhere in midnight's morning, his glow
Quickens globed lobelias, their black clefts flaring
Scarlet with his passing, drops into the clearing
Right behind the farmer's eyes, startles him
Sharp awake beside his slumbering, grim
Dream-companion, forty years. What face to show
As dawnlight thickens to noon gold? Mechanical
Thump of hooves, his slow body, and still the appall-
ing light in his head that will not leave him, why,
The new one breathing near, lips wide, scarf awry.

One moment of head-fire that sprang in the *Shopping-Bag*
Is eating his bones away: his sleeping slag
Flared to a mad resin as her hand idled across
His crocodile skin, watching her toss
A black mane sideways with a rough laugh, slam
Her hand on the till as if nothing meant a damn
And he knew, through a haze of tractor-fumes and the dragg
-ing muds of spring, he would dream of her throat
Bare and pulsing, as when she stroked his coat
And specially when she whispered: *Come back,
Old-timer, you got green oats in your gunny-sack.*

Will mean wife-widowing alive, long
Spiral down to maple-mould, mad spider-song:
Empty kitchen, bump of boot on hearth-stone,
Word scorching in the mouth unsaid, dry crone-
spittle, grackles scratching the day; will mean death
Wished for, each hour winding toward evening breath.
He feels him there again, laughing among scuppernong
Vines, in well-water singeing face, rinsing,
Why, hot limbs: *I am too old for this flensing
Fire, leave me be, plain man, I am plainsman;
Leave me be, old, in elm-shadow, where I began.*

Whistles a worn-out love-tune as he plunges,
Man of clocks, into barn-shadow, arranges
Pails, quick, locks bin-rails, feels the raw season
Rasp his hands, yelps in joy, while among frozen
Images, grandsons hung on walls, his dream-companion
Dreams on, hating the stranger, the bright one
Who ruins her history. It is no woman changes
Her world, but a god doused with grape-light.
                                                He reads
Parables in bird-song, cow breath, alfalfa seeds —
And she beside him night after night reclining
In a hell of wakefulness, his face shining.

from Five Songs for Eros

LINES FOR A TEACHER

You told my daughter what
To call you by, which she
Could not have known
For you refused ever to set it down.
This was your surprise, first day —
To smile, and breathe in each small ear:

*This is my name, which is not
My name, which everyone,
Everyone* here
*Will call me by. Children
You must pronounce it exactly as
I say.*

You did not add: *Or else
I ram you down on your young back
As one might drop a cornsack.*
You did not yell:
*Don't ever call
Me by my name my name is
Not my name.*

No. You did not jump
Immediately; waited,
A week, prepared your moment well,
And then began to yell, began
To slap and dump.

My daughter told me
Who calls things by their names,
All that you'd done.
I told her: 'Should she
Strike you, once,
For a wrong not yours, you must
Stand up and kick her hard,
Here on the shin-bone
And kick again, then
Run down the corridor
And tell them, '*Please call
My father, he is charging
Miss Jenny*' — you, Miss Jenny
Who is not Miss Jenny but
Miss Brindley, and is ill.
You must have sensed her fire,
And mine, for though you hovered
Over her, something
Checked you and you fell
On the softer ones.

I told the principal.
He shifted in his green
Swivel chair and told me nothing,
Which is the best he knows,
And shuffled off nowhere —
Where he has always been.

I told myself:
It's not the body, the delicate
Hinges of the spine, the tiny
Flutings of the ear —
Not only the body but
That burning in the mind;
The fear they sit
With every day

Of sudden error,
Of calling their new world by
Wrong names, the fear
Of a witch who has
No purpose but your terror.

I have known you elsewhere
In other guises
Loosed among five-year olds:
Balding, teeth yellow,
Whacking hands, reddening legs,
Each day drugged with the thrill
Of welts and bruises, hungry
For hatred, never to know
Sunlight in the blood,
The delight
Of strolling under the good
Trees with an easy mind.
I tell you, you have stained
This old profession:
So young, so crammed with loathing
Under your puce lipstick
The slick
Girlish hair-do.
And even if the story's true
That your father took you at five,
Then dandled you
And cooed *Miss Jenny* in your ear,
You still may choose, choose — to loathe
Vile pin-ups in a sleazy bar —
But not these. You may not breathe
Near them while
We live.

So do not come
This way again, for we will drum
You out. Tonight
Perhaps in some quiet ward you will press
Your hands, and rock as
Moonlight
Winces over the grass.

We wish you well again.
And may you choose —
Though it be difficult —
To remember yourself, and learn
Your proper name, living
Where the flowers are flowers,
The children children.
But never here.

We have grown tired of our forgiving.

SO QUIETLY

Who would have thought that you, so quietly,
Who could set any dark room blazing with
Voluptuary innocence, who froze the candy-apple
Against our teeth when Gregory Peck leaned over
And kissed your mouth, whose every movement
Kept us awake till dawn while the first fuzz
Thickened on our jowls, so heated the blood
In aging professors that they leapt over twenty
Starved years and took their astonished wives
Savagely, without a word, in kitchens and in
Sewing-rooms, right after church, their boots half on,
Turned hordes of Othello-skinned Italians
Up to the arctic riffling Swedish grammars
While you flew South to the sputterings of
A second-rate volcano, set Congress
Raging because you loved so carelessly, your thought
Plain as a running river, and as difficult,
Would rise on your birthday, late at night,
Toss back a glass of *Veuve Clicquot,* chuckle,
Stride to your room, pull up the sheet
Over your slow disease, and without a word
To any of us who in our labyrinths
Whispered always to you and only you,
Turn your face
Quickly to the dark and,
Most privately, burp, and die.

SINGLE HANDED

Here is a man examining his hands under a hurricane lamp, which he has just lit with great difficulty, after crashing in from the lake, yelling *OH, JESUS!* then, after a pause, *OH, JESUS, WHAT IS THIS?*

He needs to look very closely because, embedded between the joints of the little finger and the ring finger of his left hand is a large fish-hook. The barb is stuck through the back of his hand and pointing upward through the palm.

The person who did this to him can't help because he's lying on the floor of the dinghy from which they'd both been fishing. It happened like this: Merle, his partner, had a strike, very close to the boat, from a huge muskie and had tried, with all his force, to set the hook immediately, but the hook had torn out of the fish's mouth and into his hand instead. And now it is really set. In the confusion that followed, Merle — an old man — had slipped over backwards and struck his head on a metal thwart, and right now he is either unconscious or dead.

One further trouble: he had been fishing with a single hand anyway as the other is splinted and thickly bandaged, because of an accident at the dock two days ago.

By rowing around with one oar, in half-crazy circles through the cross-currents, he somehow got the boat back to the dock and made Merle, or Merle's body, as comfortable as he could, and then cut the metal leader from the hook by holding his fish-knife between his boots and sawing at it for so long and with so little effect that he was surprised when the metal stands eventually weakened and snapped.

Now he is staring at his hands, wondering how he managed to light the lamp — but that hardly matters. He knows there are some pliers somewhere in the shed, but it takes him a clear half-hour to find them. By that time the lamp is out and he has to re-fill it and re-light it. Another twenty minutes, and night thickening everywhere. And Merle, dead or living, must be getting cold.

He stands up, too abruptly, to listen to the sound of an outboard on the lake, and knocks the lamp over, and everything goes black save for a thin slice of moonlight through the porch doorway. He fumbles for the pliers with his right elbow and his hooked hand; finds them, then angrily kicks the door open. The moonlight widens and he squats down in it. Now he tries to get one foot between the handles of the pliers, and the other on top of the upper handle. At the same time he has to slide the barb of the hook into the mouth of the pliers, and press the top foot down, slow and hard. He wants to cut the barb off clean, and draw the shank of the hook back through his hand.

But the pliers turn over, and his hand with them. The pain explodes from the center of his palm and suffuses his whole body. It is so overwhelming that he doesn't say anything at all. He is sure now there is no one listening. He tries again. And again. And once again. And fails.

He leans back against the wall of the porch, and listens to the loons somewhere out there in the night.

This will be a helluva story when it's over. Merle will be dead, or alive. He himself will be dead from sepsis, or alive — with a beer in his hand, telling someone about it, maybe Merle.

He reaches for the pliers and decides to try the same trick again.

It's the only trick he knows.

A HOT DAY IN KANSAS CITY
1.
There must be someone breathing here.

All night these lacquered beetles
Doze against the kerb; then, in the early light,
With a click and a roar of wings
They're off,
Leaving car-shaped hollows all along the road.

There must be someone behind that door
Where the paint
Curls back in heavy sunlight.

2.
Wind in his belly, he rolls off the sheet
Head-bones humming with the voices of his sons
Who drift like smokey vines about the house.
Here they come in the citron light, smelling of sperm,
Of black foliage sweating rain. They light cigarettes.
Their feet take root in the floor.
White birds flicker over their teeth.
3.
And he up, and off, shucking away the paper;
Drags his wound outside again, a sour juice
Fumes under his heart, he snuffs the tobacco air.
Roots and tendrils burst through his house,
Through the walls of his head;
Feed on him, suck him down to nothing.
4.
Tiny cars with legs! — dark strings winding up the tree!
And these, that glint like oil-drops, sniffing each other
Winding up the thruway. Their dry carapaces
Litter the prairie, husks rolled over by the wind,
Browning under rain as the edge of the city
Chews the prairie; but the fields
Bite back — a splitting of earth,
A black and emerald wind out of nowhere, suddenly.

By Liberty Creek a house explodes. Wind breaks a truck's back,
It leaps at the sun, skews over
Wheels humming at the sky. Shiftless men
Fossick about, black ants on the plain. They sign papers.
The fields heave their shoulders, the fields know they will win.
They lie back, talcumed with phosphorous,
Stomped on by engines, and men, and medicated cows.
5.
We have eaten the prairie, and now
It works on us. It walks inside us
Scrabbling with hot hooves.
It won't lie down with us in the yellow heat
Under the music of goggled flies.
6.
His watch goes dead, his hand
Hangs from the wheel like a wet creeper.
It could be the coming of afternoon, the going of morning,

Always alone, his brain chiggering.
All is in moving, and when the traffic
Blares to a halt, the liquor climbs in his throat.
His suit grows over him like a humid skin,

The bright snake of his necktie strangles him.
He looks up, catches his whey face in the mirror —

Or was it the glass eyes of the one behind him?
7.
There must be someone breathing here!
Metal bushes rise from the roofs;
They suck images out of the sky
And splat them on the screen for someone,
Surely! For when the bushes die
Window-blinds blink once, and silence
Leans on every house.
Tonight the bushes jangle in the wind.
The actors are powdered with flickering snow,
The engines are snorting in their hollows —

And all the dark fields that surround us
Tucked in decently, laughing under the moon.

NORTH
For Michel Monnot, beginning his walk for the Parkinson Society, from Florida to Maine, May 11, 1991

The figure forms a cross, take a stick and draw it
In sand, or chalk it on a wall: one line North
The other, West. This man draws it in
Blood, heart-thumps, draws it in fire
Along thighs, down shin-bones, tempered
By pounding on roads, roads, and then, more roads.

The figure is no accident, it was this fire
Pulled his ancestors south from Burgundy, it
Clung to them as they scaled the mountain-roads
To Compostella where the North
Star watched them pay tribute to the Saint in
Prayers and amulets — some ill, some bad-tempered —

But always in passion, the roll of the roads
Under their sandals, wind-blasts from the north
Riding over their shoulder-blades. What kind of fire
Compels this man? Anger, tempered
With desire to know. What spawned it?
Sickness, hunger for a place to stand in

With pride, so that, up there in the North
He can say: *This cross is mine. These roads
Of America are in me and my mind is tempered
Steel in one thought: we will find it.
A year, ten years — what matters is we work in
Patience and friendship and urgency and fire

To find it soon!* Who will walk the roads
That this man walks? Who will share his fire?
Everyone here, and those who could not make it.
Michel, stay calm, stay even-tempered
If you can. If not, no matter — blast off in
Your own way, blast off to the North.

We in our cushioned rooms will trace the fire
-line you draw through Appalachia, going north
Where they prepare a place for you to rest in
Though rest is not your way; you are no well-tempered
Instrument, no matter which way you play it,
But a man of risks, and courage, a man of roads.

Walk with Michel on all his roads,
Temper his difficult journey to the North,
Fire him up, yell in his ear: *Yes, man, you can make it.*

MASKS

LOVERS

His Afterthought

Then, turning, she said: *Let's make love
Between two fires.* And lit the hissing gas one,
Trimmed the paraffin flame; spread rugs.
And I was reading, but she took the light.
My body tensed like a wire. And neither spoke.
Outside, a naked tree held the moon's weight
In a branch fork. Within the clock beat louder.
There was a swelling greenness in the groin
And the blood throbbed like a held bird,
And if I was eager for some mystery when
Her silks flowed to the floor — when, with a laugh,
She flung her light things to a chair —
After the sweat of it, that fathomless clutching,
Now I am hungry for familiar things,
With the burden of traffic on the solid road,
And her moist hair drowsing over my face. Some day
Perhaps I'll ask the meaning of those fires.

Her Rationale

It is by subterfuge we hold, anger, fascinate:
Say a left kerchief — or a record borrowed.
We work in the interstices of things,
In shadows where men are either gauche or noble.
Sometimes I stop short at the mirror, deploring this —
But what of his marauding, the cocky
Vanity? One must keep a grain of pride
Against this jocular raping. *Une machine à aimer.*
No, not that!
           And so: unreason, surprise. Moments
He'll pause today: *Two fires. Don't get it.*
Chuckle, lean back. *You know, women are strange.*
Then, on a whim, he'll call. And I will not say:
'There are evenings when *I* like to choose —
And I choose against this caricature you make me.'
Would follow bleak nights, gas-ring suppers, for one.
It must not be said. Hold steady. And keep
From that desert where the last trick has failed.

THE ISLAND WEATHER OF THE NEWLY BETROTHED

'The winds are more predictable in summer;
Not like that January one that banged
Off walls and clutched a cold hand at your groin
When you were forced outside. Now you can walk
With the sun firm across your shoulders
Not waiting to be shaken, or spun, flapping
Like a scarecrow. There's merely
A wavering, at dusk, in the lemon leaves,
A light lifting — and the strong one that
Drives from the sea and spins the mill-blades fast.

If this is anyone's weather it is yours —
Or part of the kindness that is yours.
Elsewhere the sun might mean silence of anger,
But today we are pleased to walk in it,
Sea all around.
                      And it will stay like this.
Unless the other thing comes, like a shock
Of impotence at noon, as when a friend
Whose words you've long admired, stares at you and
Stares, forgetting your name, dribbling
The same crude sound over and over.

Against which sudden changes we have learned
Our loving's fallible. Though not entirely.'

"Speaking of winds, I think the saddest one
Is that broad breeze in the afternoon that lifts
The gorse for thirty miles, and slides warmly
Up the face. I have been studying
Why it should sadden me: something to do
With bones, or the sense of age it carries.
Hearing September rain against the window
Or fizzing in leaves, others are moved
By something similar.
                      All that leaves me indifferent.
Still, we are too fond of metaphor.
Such moods are personal, inexplicable.
The weather has no connection with you or me.

And as for loving, I've chosen you
Because you know your stances are ridiculous.
And if one night you also lose your reason
Or puff yourself, confounding metaphor
With fact; or, when grey weather comes,
Slump, world-rejecting in your favourite chair —
Or if my body lose its tang for you,

Against those sudden changes I would say
Our loving's fallible. Perhaps entirely."

SONG OF A LECHEROUS MAN

These drifting afternoons, while others
Sweat for the general good,
We drowse and listen to the sounds
Of this tired neighborhood:

The swish and boom of traffic down
The black road — a kind
Of nascent dialect that falls
And floats on the acid wind.

And lately there's a puffed up pigeon
Patrols the ledge — a grey
Nervous one, with an eye that stares
In a queer fixity.

You turn and call me *Darling*.
Hell, if you only knew
You'd find a word more apposite!
I am no use to you

Save when I use you in this way.
You'd never understand
Why I resigned. I said to write —
But it can't be explained.

If you must know, imagine death;
A cold flame that destroys
The mind's fabric, but slowly,
Imagine your sharpest joy

Suddenly frozen, like the pigeon's
Metal stare. No, don't scan
My face like that. You'll find no love.
I'm like those crouching men

In mediaeval glasswork. You'll
Catch my expression on
The ecstatic countenance of some
Pallid god-kissing man.

No, you won't understand!
                              So sleep,
Curled in your dream of love.
For then I watch, and the flame
Rises — and that's enough.

MARRIED SONG

When you thrust out from a bewildered waking
Leaving me stupid in half-sleep, taking
Your bony warmth into the gelid room,
Beneath the covers I'm in a womb, tomb

(Or whatever accords with your philosophy)
Weaving my Morning Thoughts — all subtlety
And nuance — and while you fill the pot
Hurl smoking toast and keep the porridge hot,

I sometimes wonder in my inactive flesh
What you can make of this. Do you wish
My death, thinking, *the lazy bastard! Why*
Should I take this crude propinquity?

I squint out from the blankets and remark
Trousers kicked off in the cold, dead bottles, stark
Disorder in the shallow room — and pull
The covers over my goose-fleshed skull,

And dream again of what you must imagine
Within the context of your cold routine:
So this is love! I call it a shocking
Familiarity, a breaking

Of dignity, all soiled, all secrets spoken.
Or does some innocence find nothing broken?
These speculations leap like golden fishes
While you clump round looking for pans and dishes.

AN INVENTION

Vinnie,
You took me to your house when Mummy and Daddy
Left you a whole weekend alone
And shut yourself all night against me
Your fencer's body
Trembling as you clenched your teeth and fought
And never let me in.
And in the morning Mummy
Called from your country house and roasted me:
'How *could* you stay all night?'
And still your bit your teeth as I replied:
'Mrs. Tweed, Vinnie and I are twenty-two
And very inexperienced,
Please find another dialing tone.'

Now you have four children of your own
Groomed like racing horses — one
With a mind half-gone
From heroin, but unerringly polite
Like the English in Rangoon.
His body trembles in the night
As he reads Ouspensky in the hut
You built for him on your estate,
And he calls you *Mummy*.

Vinnie, in Paris you were betimes a snobbish bitch
But very rich
And outrageously beautiful. Have you gone
To disrepair?

The curve you made in the summer air
Always barely out of reach!
I remember the morning currawongs, thunder
Of white combers down the beach.
Three of our clever friends are eating clay
As I imagine all this, thirty years away
From the time I trod on your corgi's foot
And your impeccable manners
Pushed me from the drawing room, while the dog
Forgave me and warmed his expensive bum
By the sputtering mallee-root log
You called a fire.

Blessings, Vinnie, on all your brood
And you. We have a hundred years
Between us now and Pacific solitude.
Mummy and Daddy are gone to ground
Who had such style and were never wrong.

Your old house is covered in a throng
Of nettles, Vinnie, are you damaged with it all?

Tonight I'm listening late
To Brahms in an echoing house
In the Minnesota fall
Waiting for everything
To happen — playing God's fool again, traveling
Around my head, horse in a stall,
And I am tired of this slow declension,
This raveling, this unraveling.

FOURTEENTH HONEYMOON AT THE CAMERON HOTEL

Climb into the high bed from the oak footstool
Beside the black-haired girl-woman
Who watches you with round eyes. This is
Your fourteenth honeymoon since your house
Cracked, one child on each side howling
Soundlessly and beating hands, like people drowning
Behind glass. And then the pieces
Began to drift apart, like rafts on a gun-metal sea:
The stuff of dreams, except that
The day hung over us, with the smell
Of sodden leaves, and a few birds
Heat-stunned in a tracery of branches.

Climb up, as if you were your own patriarch
Five centuries down in the depths
Of another country, another time:
Karelia — the silence after cow-bells.
Your night-cap askew in the twilight, toes
Pinched on cold floorboards, your wife's breath
Curling up like bear-smoke in the gelid air —

As if you were your own grandfather, carrying
Root and branch in you: clowns, and wise men,
Sung at appointed times around a fire of bones.

Yes, climb up, and find yourself
Mistaken again, for you cannot conjure
Your central man, your ancient origin —
Only his voluptuary cousin, the one
They whipped from the village constantly
Especially in May when pine-resin
Hisses under the bark, and beyond the window
A neon flashing *DINO'S BURGERS*
Through a surf of pink snowfall.

Wife, womb, woman,
It's warm in here beside you,
As the world turns its back to the sun; looking
For a garden in this terrible snowlight
Where the cars swish by — a kind
Of wedding-hymn played on the ceiling:
Fighting for wakefulness, fighting to keep
The crack from widening any more.

THE SURF AT WHITNABY
Three for the Sunday Shadow

1
What are you doing, down there, head hanging
In the mirror, ringed with acanthus leaves?
You condensed out of the saffron light too early
Between the voice of the preaching-man and Brahms;
Whatever words you snapped under the wind-chimes
You know you're less than wanted and won't
Look up through the bandage of your stillness.
The roses have no mind of you, they bump
The lead-light still and still the spaniel
Yaps in a whirl of sprinklers. One more year.

I stare from the landing at your cold medallion
Face, still hungering and rehearsing, lost
By the surf at Whitnaby, rusted cannons
Aimed at wind-walls and the coast of Mars.

2

The surf at Whitnaby, like an old woman's hair:
Too many gulls in too many skeins of air
And your mind flaring with its old sorrow. Walk up!
Break from your salver of glass, come in. I've kept
Your notebook, here on the shut piano.
This is your true sonata, and this the quaver
Where courage left you like a whelp in rain
And ran, and runs till your imagination's
A thunderhead of squibs and formless fire.
Sit down square with it. You have the keys.

This is your time to sing for the beetle-mouths
That chumble your history, ranging
Among discarded diaries and broken flutes.
Strike E for this present sunlight. Begin there.

3

What draws you again to the surf at Whitnaby's
A dead man's pain who made no sound at all.
You cannot blame him for your thistle-garden
Nor the cat, brittle-boned before his time.
Somewhere between your father and your daughters,
Forgive these hands, those hands, and strike the keys.
Sing of your blindness, and your anger
Drowned in a honey-spoon; that she walked away
From your too much gentleness. Forgive three
Generations their crimped eyes and their silence.

There is no judgment day, no dark design
Except your own. Come home now, and swallow all
Your cod-liver days till they rise hard in your
Throat, black as obsidian shards bursting with grain.

MAN IN THE TRAIN

A rope of smoke winds slow
Across the wide window.

I watch it break in a fretwork
Of trees, dissolve a fence, torque

And thin over the stubble. The sun
Flares; eyes narrow in the sudden

Wash of light. This is
To meet a person whose life brushes

My life. She detains me
Lightly, surely.

I rehearse a phrase, a gesture,
Knowing there will be no cure.

And finally I am
Afraid of journeys. One is not the same.

Is either well
Again, or again ill. An old trouble.

Better to turn back. Write. Forestall
Arrival.

MONOLOGUES

PIERO, PAINTING

for Jill Ewald

Nonsense to say it's a kind of music.
Whoever heard of trumpets in the eye?

A matter of slicks and flooded gussets
That gorge into themselves a criss-cross
Of indigo magma mounds still hot
Because you slap them and slop them
Someone might suggest how the lips snarl
There across a she-ape's teeth a beached
Dolphin thrashing sand I tell them
Stretched rag, the stubborn grain of it
Now crystals whacked in fire now
Zero blue latticed against black-blue
I might concede muscle gristle fur-gobs
Caught in their own bristle but never think
Of wolves or dolphins. I want line lump
Soot-blossom this rump you call
A marmoset's. I don't. I can make
Nothing from jibbers or howls.

Listen:
The plain fact is it makes no sound at all.

SONG FROM A PLAY

Sweet curve of thigh, the neural itch
Excite the spore in our blind man's ditch:

In by the wings and out by the trap,
Dusting of lime then the sharp slap
Of a pinewood lid; a shower of pebbles
And canned bugle-music end our troubles.

In spite of that the spore hunts on
Like a cobra stretching toward the sun,
A cuttle-fish thrashing in its shell —
Or a tight couple in a pink motel.

OLOF ANDERSSON'S RUNE

I, Olof Erik Andersson,
Cut my name in this blank sand-stone
And set it in the house's root
Deep in the wall by the chimney-foot.

Back of the stone in a jam-jar
I roll my song, for no one's ear
Except my own while I survive —
And that's not long, as I believe.

Vi har oss själva, annars ingenting.

This is my story, I tell it plain
As I'll not pass by here again:
We came from the lake, the tracks rough,
The horses dying — camped at a bluff

By the big river, and then at last
We shot the horses, ate them, paced
A hundred miles to build our house
Against this hill smoothed by the ice.

My wife — eight years she shared my pillow —
Was quick, merry, thin as a willow.
I hated my sons and, as they went,
Laughed at their backs and never spent

One thought on them, nor they on me —
Gold-lovers, crooks, their fingers sly.
My daughter first, and then my wife
— I cut their marks with this very knife —

Died early. Thirty years alone,
But happy enough as I chip my stone.
The crickets are loud tonight as they sing:
Vi har oss själva, annars ingenting.

When any man dig out this song
I shall be neither right nor wrong;
I shall be dead, my bones among —
I, Olof Erik Andersson,
Son of my father, father to none.

(June 11, 1894)

AT THE EDGE OF WINTER
(Mildred Andersson, 1823-1864)

Just now I heard the screech-owl
Shiver his scale
Down the darkness, and down my spine.

His voice was older than the snow
That scratches my window
While I lie remembering:

This morning in skimble-skamble wind
I gathered the sheets with their rind
Of ice, and cracked them in my arms;

In the barn the mothering goat
Rubbed her muzzle on my throat
And, suddenly, I was afraid.

Once more, curving to his need,
I have folded his bitter seed
Within my body,

This unknown country I call
Myself, where the new one
Kicks at my wall;

Hangs there, under my heart
With a weight
I cannot shake

Neither standing in the wastes of noon
Nor resting here, where a thin moon
Flowers in the icicles.

Hard awake;
Black
World grinding among the stars.

Hard awake, and dawn
Not come, I listen to the snow sift down:
I listen to the whole house breathing.

WIFE WAITING

This the hour that seems to lose the clock,
And that stupid dog staring from the mantelshelf
Cold, and half-malign. *Sit down, then, think.*
Sprouts peeled; meat basted. This morning
You waxed the floors. And now, the dead time,
That you feared, has found you. And something's cold
Despite the radiator's red grin.

Think. This is too sudden and unreal —
Yet nothing's happened. Except hints, flickers
Of the eyes, suppressed angers. Last night
Too eager love-play, and the heart questioning —
Why do we question so? Yet something rankles
Unmentioned.
                    The child sleeps now, in the un-moving hour,
A stranger. Yesterday I smacked too hard, soothed
Too quickly, and she hung resentful,
Bewildered. I must be firm, yet kind. The middle way,
He says. I nod — with my mind.
                                   But where's the middle way
When a child attacks with a love that twists to anger,
Stamps feet, curls in a corner? Sometimes one fights
Unreasonably — or softens and is a child.
But he stands tall, rational — the necessary
Tower.
           What is it? Once my body
Met the lust in him, but the lust has trimmed now
To a respectable flame. And I hate this casting back.
But why should I yield — be a compliant wife
To smile, and smooth my dress? I have
A certain skill beyond this role
Of listening, yielding, making tea
At accustomed times. Beyond this gradual starving.

I wish he'd come. I'm tired of thoughts, shadows.
Come quickly, or stay ten years away! Put down
That thought... And yet, perhaps one has a right
To this cool solitude, and this blankness
Where the white dog stares... and I wish he'd come.

AUSTRALIAN TONGUES

Barracoutta Fisherman: Tasmania

You have to get up early, be five miles off the coast as dawn comes up over the headland. That's the best time. No one knows why. Maybe the small fish rise to the light and the big ones follow, or maybe they're hunting water-lice. Who knows? Anyway, they're always just under the surface, about half a metre down. So you take the jig-stick and you thrash the water behind the stern like a madman and sometimes while you're flailing away and all the water's white you hook one in the gills or the belly and it feels like you've got a bull on the end of your wrist.

And specially when the wind's heaving white caps all around and you hit a school. You've got six lines out and the boat's like a guitar trailing slack strings through the water. Suddenly all the strings go tight at once and you see a little fleck of foam on the end of each line dancing on the water and you have to haul the fish in against the run of the boat. Bloody hard work. And you can't stop pulling because the jig doesn't have any barbs on the hook. You gotta keep the pressure steady right up to the boat then swing him up out of the water into the tank then flick the jig back fast. One movement, and when the line snaps taut you start hauling again.

Last week we worked like that — three hours in a single school and I remember thinking what a terrific sound it'd make if you could pluck all the strings at once, and the whitecaps bobbing and the wind howling. Jesus, it was beautiful.

It's up and down a' course but it's a livin. I been round 'coutta boats since I could walk. Built this one last year, every plank. You know, when you rub your hands against a boat you built yourself, it's like a living thing, and last night we we're coming down the estuary near dusk and all around the boat there was this green fire in the water-weed and I looked up at the light falling behind the island and it all seemed old as if you were seeing it again for the first time and it was all ending — or maybe it was all beginning.

Opal Miners

Dumb bastards, living down here — just for bits of fire.
Weasels in a hole. Last week a truck
Went past, we heard it shake the ground.
Truck, I said. *Herb, it's a truck.*
I don't think Herb understands most words
Any more. We never speak, just dig. Hardly ever.
But he heard the shaking too
So we both up into the horrible daylight.
Blinding white, musta been 40. And there was
This truck, stopped, still tickin over
And a big fella with one of them army helmets
And a great handkerchief droopin down his back.
Lookin straight at us, through binoculars
Like we was animals or somethin.
Just lookin, maybe five minutes.
None of us moved. Herb, me, nor him.
Then he put the glasses down, and you know
What he did? Give us the finger.
Then he dropped down and they drove off.
Not a wave, not a bottla steam. Only the finger.
Just as well he didn't speak, I s'pose.
Herb's no good with strangers.

And I'm better off down here lookin for
Whatever I'm lookin for. It's slow,
But it beats Sydney any day. And when you find
A good one even Herb starts jabberin.
And I think to myself, *that's what we came here for:
Little lost fires.*
                            Look, if I carry them
Up into the light and hold them you can hear
The big fire, and the little ones, here
On my open hand, all talking to each other. Maybe
That's why Herb don't trust ordinary words any more.

We'll probably stay here till we croak.
By then we'll have almost no use for them.

Only a handful, one or two each year.

Post Graduate

I have this disease: three-letter word.
Not Ph.D.
                There we were — in the end just six of us;
Too much Kierkegaard and Derrida.
Wired on coffee, very elite, jawing in the Caf.
Richard went off to Oxford to write his thesis on
Whether a surface can be red and white all over.
After a year I sent him a post-card: *'Well?'*
Another year — then he replied, *'Can't exactly say.'*
About that time I looked down at my body:
Pale as a fish-belly, cold. I'd been reading
Until my eyes were back in their caves and smouldering.
Kierkegaard's disciple. What for? Everything
Seemed flat: the harbour water, travelling, words.
Somewhere in all the words I'd lost what the Greeks
Call *achiote*: my own sharpness.
I was like a hot wire dancing on a lawn.

Some of us looked for causes: Ethiopia, the Greenies.
I graduated to painting, and this immaculate room.
I'm supposed to be unhappy. Last weekend
I ran my second marathon,
And finished four booming canvases. Sold them all.

My house is full of plants and old books —
Books that I read — my cellar stocked
With Margaret River, Barossa, Rutherglen.
All aged, nothing tawdry.

But I was speaking about the disease.

I like them when they laugh on time.
If they do it too early, I send them home too early.
Too late's almost as bad. I like detachment.
But not indifference, not big boys running from themselves.
Put it this way: a sense that we move in our own waters,
An old dignity. Angophora limbs. Stars.
But where we touch I think we should be kind.
It's not exactly Celtic, the tribe
Singing in four parts round the camp-fire.
Judicious, though, selecting from the possible:
How days might go, and nights also.

I choose well, have chosen well. Not
Rigid, but very sure, and sure that I will die.
Meanwhile, no one buys me. But I *can* be
Irrational about a shapely bum. The rest's all private.
As with the deepest cabernet — charnu, velouté —
You have to earn the favour.

DENTIST AT WORK

Mister, if I could illustrate this moment
What a refuse-pit you yawn under my hand,
What sliming heaps of calculus and sagging gums,
And what richly stinking caries these bicuspids house,
You'd squirm in raw embarrassment, not pain.
No. 4, please, nurse. And a matrix band, upper jaw.
My arrogant professor would have protested:
'I'm no sanitary engineer. Chew pumice.
And come again.' A deeply arrogant man.
But I'll scrape; clean; restore. Try to sweeten it.
Probe, please. Open wide. Perhaps you've a wife.
Christ, even my hardened stomach twitches
At that! Gingival rot, both jaws. Gums
Suppurating. Pretty.
                      These teeth
Bit solid once. *No 3 burr, nurse. Have a rinse.*
I'm cold now. Balancing forces: health; pain;
Filth. This toxin seeps to your toes, is drained
By your stomach. Headaches, listlessness; lose
Your spunk. Can't run a dozen yards, I'd wager. A flaccid
Thirty-year old, lounging about weekends,
Inert as a cushion. Diets of whisky, cakes
And creamed potatoes. Sucks lollies in the train.

Open wide. Open very wide, mister. This is a fight.
You think me silent; cruel perhaps. Nothing to say.
But if at some garrulous party you should ask
Why I pursue this trade, excuse my shrug
And my simple answer: health, even
In the place of eating — and of kissing — is still
A kind of health. *Open up. Not long now.*

LEICHARDT IN THE DESERT

I did not choose to make this westward journey
Into the dry rock country of the dead
Where in the torpid light the lizards
Flick from our tracks into the mean rock shadows;
To slash that tunnel through the mountain forest
Cross the grasslands, wade the inland rivers
I did not choose; say, rather, I was called,
By a voice that followed in restricted
Avenues, stopped me in doubt before my window;
Grew louder, more insistent — till I came.
And now our sullen band proceeds
Into a wilderness of hard-leaved bushes.
We have turned from the cities of our birth:
We spit on the memory of those violent cities:
And we are bound in a hate that has no symbol,
Hating each other's sickness in ourselves.

Our feet kick dust, the whitened bones of animals,
And of men, and our expressionless eyes
Gaze toward the distant dragon-back of mountains
Which is perhaps our destination —
And that thought racks us with a marvelous fear.

I do not know these men. I shall preserve
The strangeness. That way, control.
Hate, sorrow, fear; these three unite us.
Bronze light beating on the gibber plain;
Dust in the mouth. Dreaming of coastal rivers,
The wheeling of the hawk; haunted by images
I must destroy, of lushness, plenitude — vines
Latticed with mellowing light. The mind's profligacy ..

You mad saints who claim to know this place
Make prayers for those on a dry journey:
Pray that our arrogance does not fail
In this hard light, in this astringent beauty.

THE HIRED MAN'S RETROSPECT OF WINTER

That winter past, troubled by the death fear,
I kept alone, avoided the others' eyes.
I remember this many-roomed house breathing wind
In odd corners, and all things seemed ridiculous
In the critical cold; the woman held to her room by sickness,
The kitchen empty, and alive with whispers.
Sometimes I'd hear the scurry of a rat
Stop; and there was a loose tile would rock in the wind.
But neither sound nor emptiness could purge
The black fear in my guts — nor the token courtesies,
The unaltering chores: wet chickens pecking
The muddied wheat-grains that I scattered
In the pooled dooryard; the sway-backed cow
Thumping along the track to the milk-shed.
An old friend, a wry Dominican, used to advise:
Cling to the holy fact in times of trouble.
There were facts enough; it was the whole
Seemed constantly unreal.
                         In the extreme weather
The twisted elms'd thrash the roof; or the days
Hold static — frozen of any meaning
I could project as I shuffled about odd jobs.

In the whitewashed barn tarantulas
Hung from furred legs, breathing, studying me
With cold eyes; and once among some seawrack
I kicked against a cat stripped smooth by wind
And surf, his legs skyward, his jaw clamped
In a white snarl.
                 And I remember the child
Lowering over his brother, a metal toy
Clenched in his hand, ready to jab
At the forming skull — except I jumped out
To grip the arm, and grip; and I watched the flesh
Throbbing in the small head, and was afraid.

And as the June days flow about us
Like a clear width of water, the images come back
With a different poignancy; my hand will falter,
And despair leap in my body. Those days
I keep alone, trying to retch it out;
But it is lodged too well.
                                Today, as I rest
Against this tractor-wheel, smoke threads out
Straight from the roof; feathers, high up.
The June days flow. As we move, cramping
A shutter split by that wind, stitching bags —

While the wheat-stalks slowly lengthen. Learning
A kind of active patience in the soul —
Or where these modulations have their ground.

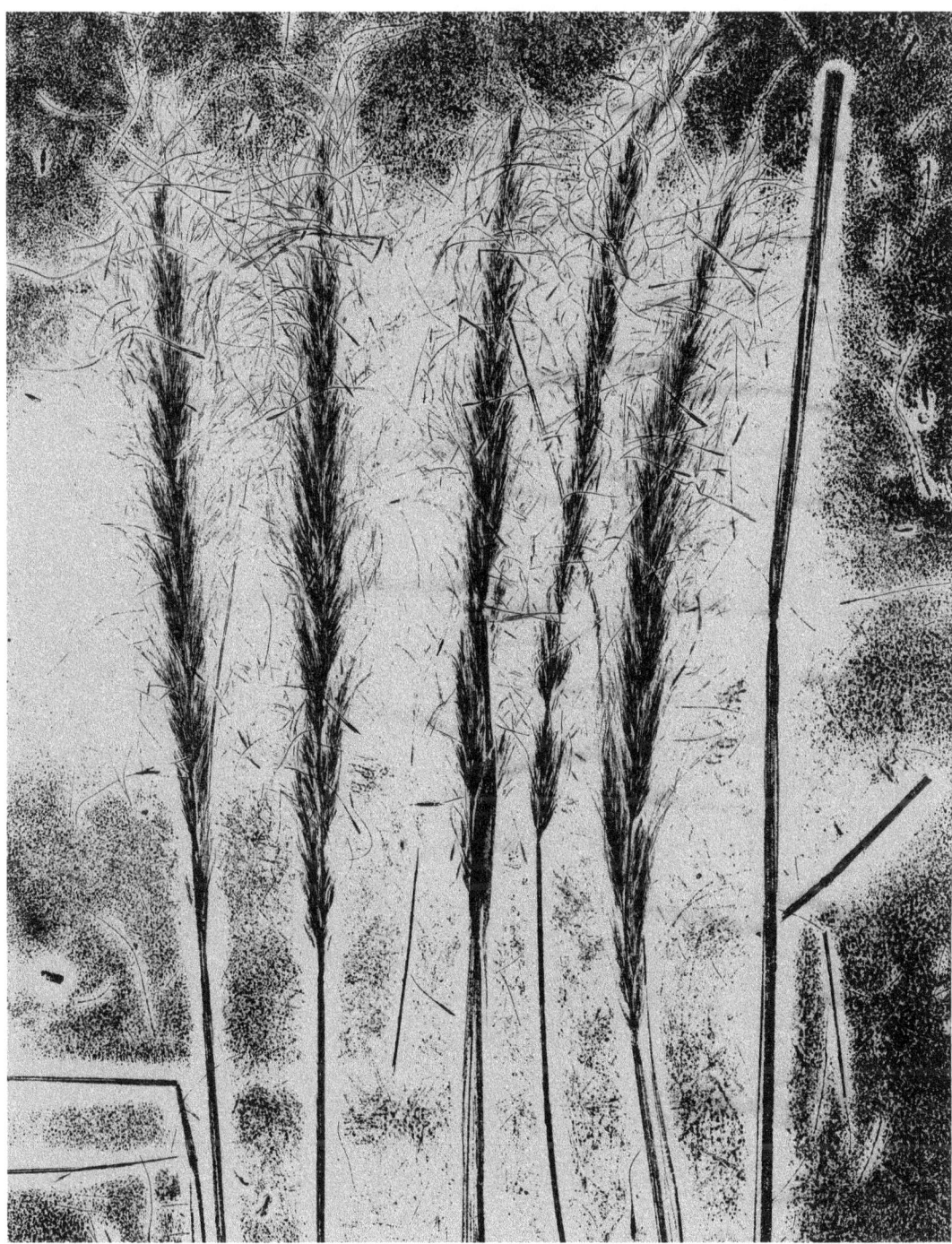

ORCHARD POEMS

A BURNING OF APPLEWOOD

Here we are in our hot boots, the fire
Stoked high, all our sins on us and our fur burning.
What a harvest we had of it!
We tramped the fruit-rows summerlong
The smell of mulch thick in our clothes.
So many centuries of mud and apples —
Like Ludovico's peasants, feet stogged
In their Sienese earth, flat on the wall
Six hundred years. Brilliant planes,
High over, trail white feathers in the sky,
Lebanon withers in flames, out of ecstasy
And murder Islam rises in the desert.
What is this peculiar stuff, water or fire,
Floods over us? Did we choose these bitter clocks
That chomp our days?
★

Your fortieth year fell yesterday. I saw you hesitate
There, at the door, then move like a doddard
A half-step, before you turned and smiled, in your eyes
A grey song that your time is winding down,
The apple-trees flecked with obdurate snow, wind
Bitching against the pane. We watch
Our children growing into their shadows,
Silent under a snow-bitten tree, while the dog
Drags his hurt paw across the threshhold.
★

The trees are ours but we will never own them.
We cut them back, pluck off the fruit, their liquor
Stains our tongues. I do not understand
The language of aphids, black beetles that flash
Their rainbow backs in the yellow light. These moments
Are given, then something carries them away.

★

Handel was taken with the exactest ways
A theme could change and change and always hold,
And Monet could never fix the light
That played across his waterlilies
Though he paint till time go black again. Today
I watch the light curve down a booming wave,
Amazed and maddened by its single repetition
As it spumes all ways in the wind.

★

I have given up parsing the volatile verbs of love.
Here are our bodies
Glistening after bathing, yours ivory
And lithe, mine stocky work-horse that bears me well.
And here's Responsibility, and Money —
A roof that needs repair. Good nouns.

★

The rhetoric crumbles in the end, goes down in the dump
With old paint-cans and busted wardrobes,
Kewpie dolls grown obsolete by staying young.

Some afternoons the silence washes over us
Like a mallow sunset in a room without music.
We stand in that quiet
Light and gradually burn.

★

    Branches click in the starlight.
    There are creatures
    Snuffing our roots. The brandy glows
    And spreads its fumes, the applewood
    Crackles with a bright malevolence.

DAWN IN CALIFORNIA

Exactly at four o'clock
  Wet light
 Spread on the lady bug
   In the country of my hand
 The eucalypt stood up on the hill
       And exactly at four o'clock
Like a white cat in the stubble
        The new song came
 It was no virgin with scrubbed feet
    It was no little boy drooling sugar
   It was the music of wet light
Spreading very quietly
      On grass and rooftop
  And happy and alone
         I turned on my side
  And swallowed it
     And slept with it coiled in my throat
   Till the damsons rubbing my window
       Exploded in the sun.

DUNG BEETLE

Thrums in his midden-mound
Opal wings
Flaring scarlet and blue:

Working for his supper.
It all tastes good to him
And to his children;

This one a delicacy
Dropped by the gangly foal
Just before dawn

That now, at noonday,
Hums and steams with a fire
That has him burrowing fast —

Tiny wart-hog
His engine-song
Drifting up, to mingle

With the dry
Cicada-drone
In the windless elm.

Look at his black metal
Shine as he clicks
His jaws making the food-chain

Firm again, while the sun laughs
And splatters his armor with
Fresh light, whose never heard

Of Jason, or Achilles.

BALLAD *

Susan and Billy and Helen and me
Went climbing. We got apples.
We got a bucket of sloppy lemons
And whammed them against the chicken-shed.
With every *whump*
The chickens went crazy.
Helen ran home and stole some cakes
From a secret jar in her mother's place.
Billy got sick and we showed him how
By poking your fingers down.

We went to the river and cut the rope
That tied my uncle's rowing boat
And shoved it out with a branch.
The current pulled us down a mile
Before we got back to the bank.
Billy was white.
We left the boat in the mouth of a creek
And hurried home, and once I yelled:
Shut up, Susan, it was all our faults.

Behind the shed in the raspberry canes
We got undressed and looked at ourselves.
Helen's tits were bigger than Susan's.
I got all stiff and Billy tried too,
Then Helen and I ran off.
I kissed her a lot in the dust and grass
And knocked her glasses off. Her little
Red thing looked like a wound and
She closed her eyes. My hand
Smelled salty all afternoon.

Billy and Susan found us there,
Their eyes went down:
What were you doing, we looked for you?

We came down here to — talk for a while.
Wanna go swimming?
                                Yeah, let's go!

Susan and Billy and Helen and me
Went swimming. We had the sand to ourselves.
We dived and ducked all afternoon,
We dived and ducked till the water
Went like a mirror, then went black,
And we were cold — cold as a bullfrog
Billy said.

We all climbed into our pants and shirts
And raced to the shed to get our shanghais.
I heard my uncle's car in the drive
And Billy whispered, *let's hide from him.*
We climbed in the shed among the rafters
Old tractor-bits and milk-machines
Where the spiders grow. We found
A basket of mouldy eggs and a giant
Freezer, and climbed in there
To hide from him.

Helen smelled salty and Susan shivered
So I held us all and kicked at the door,
And nothing moved, and I said
Nothing in the dark.

Susan and Billy and Helen and me
Went climbing. The apples
Shone in our hands, the lemons
Bammed on the chicken-shed. And once
I swam to the top of the tree
And saw the river winding out to the sky.
Then Billy dragged me down.
                                                      We slid

Like fish in the yellow water and then
My uncle came and I said *We*
Stole your apples and he looked strange
As he picked me up, his mouth was
Swimming but I couldn't hear him Oh

Susan and Billy and Helen and me
Went climbing the water ran fast
Through the yellow apples and Susan
Grabbed me and Billy screamed
We'll never — and then his breathing
Stopped and the black thing came.

And then you opened the door
On Susan and Billy and Helen and me
And then you opened the door
And Susan and Billy and Helen and me
Were high in the apple-tree, and we
Were dreaming.

* *After a poem by Roland Flint. See note, p 358*

THE SENSE OF FALLING

You're dozing there, four hundred feet
Above the city, stretched out on a red T-bar;
Your lunch-tin under your head, you dream
Of bright waves slithering up the rocks,
The noon sea amethyst and cobalt.
You breathe slow and full, the taste of banana in your throat.
The sound of traffic floats up, faint thunder,
Your boots rubbing three pale stars.
You smile, and turn toward your lover, reach for her hair —
And hurtle from your frame, your lunch-tin breaks open,
The lid spins up and away like a coin in water,
And now you flail in a wind that you create, eat wind
4.19 seconds, then hit hell floor and blackness,
And you will never touch your lover's face,
Will never walk that beach, seawind mussing your hair —
And cannot tell how your rise on the long pole
Of your daughter's voice, to coffee-smells,
The cold floor pressing under your soles —
Nor how you pluck this apricot, break it
Against your teeth and stroll the fruit-rows
Where brilliant beetles, looking for cracks in the wind,
Ride the branches on their spiky hands.

LAST EVENING

1

My friend Verconi keeps a black machine that squats
All summer on his verandah rail. Each night
It glows, and waits for the sound of wings.
When a yellowjacket or a bloated fly
Floats near, like a heavy comma,
The crimson filaments invite them in.
Inquisitive, they brush the grille; then,
With a withering zap of smoke and boiling juices
They roast — no time to modulate their music,
No time to bargain or remember.

We lounge by the edge of the wide verandah
Clinking cubes in our glasses, talking
Of vegetables and politics. Intermittent
Whiffs of scorched bodies; quick buzzes
Like shocks from a pinball machine.
At last we rise for dinner. The table
Holds cool forks, and watermelon rounds.

2

The walls of Verconi's bathroom are ablaze.
If I could push out this pane of red-hot glass
I'd see a bicycle against a fence, two trash-cans,
The roofs of ordinary houses in the dusk.
But I am locked inside this room — all the water
I flush into this basin can never wash
The red light off my skin nor cool my hands.

3

We take dessert by the verandah-rail.
The small talk grows smaller. Each act is
Provisional: they have counted all the seconds.
The last light filtering through the maple
Etches our faces with a tawny fire.
This is Minneapolis, and anywhere.

Our instruments have shrunk the world
To a rainbow bauble that floats up
From a child's pipe. Verconi's boys
Do not speak, but peer at the screen
And blast each other's spacecraft into blackness.

Smell of coffee, smell of insects burning.

My eyes track the flight of a dusty bird
To an old crab-apple by the junk-shed.
Bitten by deep winters,
The tree won't quit, but once more
Presses its tart fruit into the dangerous air.

NOT QUITE ITHAKA

> *The roaring wind is my Wife, and the Stars through*
> *my window-pane are my Children.*   John Keats

Home by myself in my draughty house
November snow splatting down:
Wet stuff that slides off the apple-boughs.
Two nights ago I stopped a fat raccoon
In the headlights as
He toppled a trash-can: black
Ears of a fox, jewel eyes
White-circled like a clown's.
Then he melted back
Into the sleeve of darkness. Today I look
For a hairy smudge on the white
Page of the paddock.
Nothing — only the snow-plain
Spreading all around. This quiet —
Save for the squeak of my wet finger
Against the window-pane —
Is ten miles thick.

And so I welcome myself to my house again.
I built this bed —
Great yawning thing
Too vast for any couple, three times too wide
For a bachelor's narrow sleep;
Built it of pitch-pine and cheap
Plywood, bought
At a country auction, years ago.
The bolts don't match. I've knocked it
Apart too often — once in Toronto,
Twice for garrets in this town.

Now it's grown
Into the conscience of the house — not
Grafted, though, to any olive-root, nor
Decked with damasks of Indian-tooth design.
Oddly, the sherbet-bearers who used to float
At evening through the door
To lay me down and soothe my limbs with oils
From Nineveh and Samarkand
Don't come by any more.

Being too idle to unbolt the thing again
I shall maybe die in it,
But maybe not today.
                       Above it, a great
Painting by Pieter de Hooch:
A woman and a snivelling kid
In a courtyard, 1658.
Deftly placed, every flag and brick
Burns clear in the moist light. The broom,
Obedient to the painter's fabulating eye,
Leans correctly on the wall.

The courtyard door frames
A second woman. White
Paper surrounds them all.
The print's buckled, it curls from the masonite.
The whole thing's wrongly
Angled.
                Beside it
The window frames the golf-hut
From where all summerlong they putt
On the opulent green. Summer's gone underground;
The workmen keep indoors today, honing
Purple hands.
                   Here I am, in my
Fiftieth year, in the wastes of white
America. Something has slid away.
I wait for the voices of my daughters — who might
Flounce in, snow in their hair,
Any week now. Meanwhile, it's me
And the raccoon — he's out there somewhere, surely.

Home, but not quite Ithaka, where the waves
Churn shingle up the yellow shore —
Not quite, not quite. But since —
Pace the story of your
Perpetually renewable Ulysses, who,
After the thrumming of the harp had stopped
And all the color drained from the day, propped
Himself against that olive-root
And fought the queer taste
That thickened in his throat
And died unsinging, a prince
Of absences — since
I have chosen
To arrange things in this way,
I am the husband of these frozen
Fruit-trees, these minutes
That drip from the eaves
And it seems, quiet mister,
That it must do, it must
Exactly do.

SUMMER POEM
for Dorothy
1
You buried your mother
Under the belly of the hill.
You did not ask permission:
Carried her there, hacked out a hole
And planted her,
Then planted a plum-tree over her.
Each year you light a ring of candles
And sing the songs she cared for.
You sing in joy, standing on
Her body, and the song goes down from your toes
And into her bones, the city
Of insects and minerals and living things
She is quietly becoming.
2
I woke this morning thinking of her
Whom I never saw.

Last night, a hungry deer
Dragged at her tree
With his blind teeth, and killed it.
You laughed when you saw the toothcuts:
She would have enjoyed his hunger —
The animal, obeying himself.
You will plant another tree in her:
Crab-apple, cherry — they'll bloom,
Or the deer will savage them.
Let it be.
   3
Our daughters bloom
In the late
Sunlight and water splashed
On their quick bodies.
Stripped off our stale clothes
Plunged with them
Down to the floor of the dark pool
Among the mud-slime and the pecking fish
Rose up blowing spray
Rinsing the shadows from our brains
Roved like dolphins through
The blue space of summer,
Enjoying hunger
Work of our hands and backs
Belly of the cow pulsing
Against our cheeks,
The house climbing the hill like coral
The white moon striding over us
As we slept with the crickets in the juicy grass.
   4
Woke this morning, thinking
Beauty is, *yes,* of body.
A thousand books fell from my mind,
Leaving only the pattern on the pinewood ceiling.
Thought of the deer's teeth,
Our daughters, their small
Breasts budding, their shyness —
And then we walked on the living grass
Over your mother's body
Over the bones of many people —
Mothers and sisters and exhausted soldiers —
Over all our brothers sleeping under the hill.

YOUNG BEARS IN AN ORCHARD

   Just as my hand goes round
       This apple, just so, we took each other
     She having turned toward me
         Firmly at dawn, while half asleep.
   Later, with a sharp lust
She bit, breaking the apple —
       The juices flew:
   We laughed like honey-bears
     And licked
       In raffish pleasure.
There is no other source than this;
       The hunger
     Walks away, there comes
        The gentlest burning.

         Here is evening;
      Our bodies, the bare stars.
       And once again
     I am hard awake, she having
      Turned toward me in
       A flame of moonlit
         Apple-flesh under
           The black boughs.

HERE

The day was still as honey in a bowl;
The maple-sap came fast, with winter gone
The cattle stood beside the bright snow-pool
Their dung packed down and steaming in the barn.
No help for it — go get your fork and spade
For even those who serve the world with wit
Are trundling down into the deep barn-shade
And blocking up their nose, and shoveling it.
You hacked and grunted all day at my side;
And then we heaped it, drove it up and flung
Great cartloads on the cornfield, near and wide,
Breathing new air rich with earth and dung.
Then stood a little while, single and whole.
And the day still as honey in a bowl.

Poems from
SONGS FROM THE DRIFTING HOUSE
1972

THE FALLOW SEASON

for Paul Ritchie

These shadows moving over new-ploughed land
Prefigure a meaning which we darkly guess.
Under our feet where once the tall crop waved
The earth lies bare save for these yellow stalks
Protruding at odd angles from the furrows;
These, and a few wet leaves that flap and scurry
Along the fitful wind, are the last signs
Of the strong, swaying harvest; for
This is the quiet time, the fallow season.
Ignorant men who pass will nod their heads,
Saying: *That earth is sour* — and turn away
Because no lushness springs to gratify
The sense, and hold indoors, keeping a sullen
Fire, inwardly cursing the unyielding weather.

And while the white rain beats across the hills
It's desolate enough. But you, who by
Some shrewd perversity or courage, toughen
On disappointment, will come through this
To make again. This is the quiet time.
Put down your brushes and your words,
Breathe with the earth, draw strength from solitude.

BLIZZARD

The drift climbs them higher and higher,
The whole field blows pale.
Broken cornstalks hung on a wire:
The hordes at Passchendaele.

A WORD IN DECEMBER

Think of that disenchantment, that sharp breaking
Out of the double darkness which we knew —
Was love the unspoken word, renewed in waking,
The cold flame that we tasted, being two —

For in that abstract world, the day's confusion,
The clear antinomies of fire and ice
Dwindled and blurred: sprang out no quick conclusion,
Yet, as I read, these images stayed precise:

Your laughter, and your warm hands — your breath, whitely
Curling against the frosted pane; the bare
Trees we saw in the white park, still as the air —

Some say winter's the death of love. If so,
What in your voice, so strongly and so lightly
Touched me just now with a flame that burns like snow?

TWO VARIATIONS ON A GROUND

1

That scrawny bird twitching on a cracked wing
Down on the smooth tiles by the chimney pot
Is like some battered poem which cannot
Get up from the flat page, get up and sing,

But in a dumb frenzy attempts to gather
Itself into its firm original form
And sags, bewildered after the brief storm —
Poor nondescript thing, broken by that weather;

And while the torn song flames within my throat
I scan the words I jabbed across the page:
Figures of haste and indiscriminate rage
Fighting themselves — and not one lucid note.

Out of the quarrel with ourselves we make
High-sounding hymns to inexactitude,
Or in a fine self-pity, brood and brood —
Well, get up, dreamer! Go out and break

Road-stones — or drive a bus. Or, if you dare,
Take each word and have it unfold and span
Precisely, leaving — like the bird down there,
Slow time to mend all else as best it can.

2

There's a pigeon twitching on a snapped wing
Down on the smooth tiles by the chimney-top;
Acts like a clockwork thing, hunches up
And hobbles, but can't straighten out and swing

Down to the trees — but once more tries to gather
Itself into its firm original form:
A dazed survivor of the harsh storm
An hour ago — smashed by that mad weather.

Consider this: to get beside that bird
I'd have to climb down ninety steps
Travel a furlong, climb again. Perhaps
The man beneath the roof'd find me absurd

(Keeper of cats, maybe, or a pigeon-eater) —
Not worth the walk and the embarrassment.
 And look, he flaps more briefly, is nearly spent.
And he will die there, starve unseen in the gutter.

And when the Yang-tse jumps its banks how many
Are flushed from their flimsy houseboats and drown?
Each of them has a body like my own,
And sum of my grief is less that one brown penny.

And yet this one bird has me staring again
Because whatever arithmetic you use
This is my field (and this I did not choose)
And I am radial to his fear and pain.

It is a sight to make brave youngsters laugh,
Look at him jerk!
                    Cursing his clumsiness
I turn away to take my bath and dress,
Half-angry with myself, and less than half.

NINE FOR A WASP AT LUNCHTIME

1

A quick dart and an abrupt stop,
Wings driving, sound of a flung top
On boards, his tigered arse turned up

Angrily, somewhere in the haze;
At which, one stiffens, crinks his eyes,
Slaps at it with *goddam flies!*

At the next table, chin near dish,
A woman dreams and feeds, her flesh
Vague in the sun. If he wished

He could crack this torpid calm
With a flung back chair and a scream
Of pain. No such alarm;

Wasp waits in the unmoving leaves.

2

Is it the wasp sings at my ear
Or the slow wine in my head? I hear
Your voice but cannot grip the meaning.

I keep nodding because your tone
Requires assent or animadversion —
But logic's in the bottom of my glass.

I started early, it damns me as a guest.
I read it in your eyes: *This is the last
I eat with him.* Your troubled eyes.

My slow words cling to my tongue.
I Brando with them, leave a phrase hang.
Your anger pricks, your voice stops.

You gaze into sea-dark wine.

3

How does the word *banana* mean
This object in my fingers?
I break it, the ends won't stick:

Banana, broken; wounded.
Scholars say I only eat
The substance. Essence remains.

Quest is essence of banana.
That's not a topic! Think.
The lady watches me

With plural eyes. Look out,
The wasp! Crawls on the skin
Jumps out and sings

Dry hymns over the ruptured fruit.

4

A story then:
              I met a man once in the dawn
And when he neared I saw his eyes
Were fixed on nothing, they were ablaze

With nothing — or perhaps some ecstasy
Which made him mad. However it was
They showed no recognition

Of the world or me, though he passed
So close I could have clutched a sleeve
To steady him. Stranger still,

He thrust both hands up to the sky,
Clenched tight as prunes, and from his throat
Came a single high syllable

                  in an attenuated cry.

5

Sometimes I catch that white face
When my mind hovers on the edge of sleep.
And the cry — like an extreme

Of affirmation and denial,
As if he'd stumbled upon the final
Grunting vowel which, bitter and clear,

Resolved for him then what mystery
Joke, or non sequitur he found
The world. A speculation:

Surely he was rammed with grief,
Or happiness — or nothing.
A cry like the death of a god.

Or a man.
                In London, years ago.

6

I shall strut for you, I shall isolate
Music of solitude perhaps.
Look I could go between these tables

Winding a terse mimetic dance.
You see we need another language
Utterly silent

Such as the crazed Nijinsky made.
My words stick to my tongue, and still you talk
Of America, *tout ça, tout ça,*

While I sit here hungering
To out-dance Nijinsky, make a superb
Figure — knowing that I'd only

Slam sideways if I quit this chair.

   7
You must excuse me, there's a place not far;
And take no notice, this has been known before.
And here, and here, and here and here

My feet outstrip their tall intelligence,
Resist the tipped world, prop my head
And the wasp perhaps! He's come inside!

Buzzes in the rubbish, I'm swollen with it,
Rubbish of the grape and rubbish of the sea
Rises. *I am a flicker of wit*

Over a swill where a drowning wasp
Waggles his legs and lives. YES, SIR! And now.
And now. Rubbish be. Humble. Has happened

Before. It has been known before.

   8
Sometimes, especially when the wind
Quits the island inexplicably,
As the nerves brace, or because

Of that — the sea going smooth — all things
Assume their differences;
A barefoot boy tamping the dust

Yells an obscenity, and grins. Somewhere,
Far off, a water-wheel creaks in the silence.
Things are themselves, and you acknowledge

Their variousness. The tree's only a tree,
The wasp an insect, that can sting.
This comes at any time — with morning at

The yellowest light, or when the late sky deepens.

9

There is a moment in a wineglass
When all men are troubled and alone.
And that's a moment when a man might choose.

All right, I guzzle wine and blur my wits.
But, that aside, I fight with words.
And you, in a loud alley of Madrid

That smells of garlic and rancid oil —
You straighten limbs and heal the muscles
Of damaged men. Words and flesh.

I choose the pleasure of resistant things;
One is sustained at last by these
Living textures, words and flesh — these always

Tough particulars.

COLLECTED SONGS

SONGS OF LARA AND THE BELLARINE (1997)

Geoffrey

When Geoffrey plays the flute
The birds at Serendip give over;
Warlock, shaman, showman, lover,
The glottal magpies and carking crows
Delight in his runs and arpeggios:
They shut their eyes
And you hear them say: 'That's beaut!'
When Geoffrey's fingers riffle the keys
Of his silver flute.

When Geoffrey drives his van
Along the roads and lanes of Lara
Waving *Hi* to Craig and Sarah —
So many friends — from Flinders Peak
To Rippleside and Lollipop Creek —
And every kid
Shouts at his blood-red Kombi
As he forges forward, like a squid:
'Hey, Mr. Dombie!'

When Geoffrey strums his chords,
— So many countries, so many songs
No one can say where he belongs,
Corio, France, or Timbuktu — his mind
Is four times wider than the wind.
With bongo or veena
When Geoffrey's tunes his words
We pause because his ear is keener
Than any bird's.

A Widow of Wild Dog Creek

Five years, and still the ash-trees and the ferns
Sound with his voice as I wind alone
Down Wild Dog Road, by the giant rock
We picknicked on, whose skin still burns
Under the slanting April sun.

Once more, I pause to watch his stallion cross
By the rock-shelf where the creek wobbles
Between dark roots and the water swirls.
He climbs the steep bank, snatching grass.
This is the place, among these pebbles,

This is the place where I let him go:
I flung him away as one flings a dice;
In white handfuls I cast him loose
On Wild Dog Creek and watched him flow
Toward King Island, and the ice.

For months, an absence like a massive bell
Not ringing through a yellow daze;
I hated moonlight, the turning sky,
The bawl of lambs; hated the shrill
Cicadas drilling in the haze.

He was my music. I hear his words
In all the wildflowers when they flare
And wither in this lovely valley;
I hear him in the banter of birds,
In silence, and the glass-blue air.

He is so close today that I can smell him.
But the agony has gone, and the farm's
My home again. What could I say
This morning, what could I tell him,
When I held my grandson in my arms,

When he turned his eyes on me and, in a flash,
I saw my husband, heard his laugh
As he gazed on every living thing.
I felt my husband rise from his ash:
We are his joyful epitaph.

Old Ted

Today old Ted is eighty-four;
He's angry with himself, and more:
Angry because the six o'clock sun
Reminds him that he's almost done.

His hair thinning, his eyes red;
His wife toppled, then she was dead.
His sons turned sour, then drove away,
Leaving Ted with the empty day.

If we were wise we'd pray for Ted
As he cranks his body out of bed.
For fifty years he loved the clean
Pipes and dials of his machine.

Now he's stopped the machine runs on
Churning fumes to blacken the sun;
Look how they climb over Avalon!
That smoke is us, what we have done.

Today old Ted is eighty-four,
An angry man who knows what for.
Breakfasts alone, the sun roars in
Revealing cracks on his lizard skin;

He drives off fast to meet the boys;
Same old wisecracks, same old noise.
We haul our buggies from green to green.
Smoke drifts over the Bellarine.

Francesca

While Daddy chops and Mummy hums
I take my clothes off and I run.

My doggy's name is Christmas Pie
I pull his tail off every day.

But every night when my room goes dark
He sleeps very hard and his tail comes back

We had a cat but he's not here,
I poured my breakfast in his ear.

One day my Daddy found a snake.
He tried to bang him with a stick.

My name is 'Cesca, I'm almost three.
What's your name, Mr Whiskers?

King of the Gallery

What moves, is what I say:
Frame it, pack it, and ship it,
Make all the phone-calls pay.

Moon-faced is what I hate,
That wounded look, that pallor.
They want it all on a plate.

Nine Views of the Bellarine:
All fodder for the eye-ball;
Sea-scapes, a bushland scene —

I say, okay if it moves,
Okay if it swells the kitty
Who cares who disapproves?

Without my walls they're dead.
Four weeks is what I hang them.
What's left I dump in the shed.

I eat, therefore I deal.
Space by time equals money.
Forty percent. It's a steal.

The Winemaker's Winter Song

When I first felt the white wind slide
Up my face with a salty flame
Watching sail-boats rock on the tide
I knew exactly why I came.

Loam drew me and the promised fume
Of yeasty Merlot as it steeps;
The tannin-tang of young wine-spume;
It was dawnlight — the way it leaps

Corio Bay in one broad flare;
And when I smelled this mud-brown earth
And rinsed my lungs with the driven air
I could already see this hearth

Where the loud fire blazes in our wine.
Fifteen summers. Come here, look
At the long rows, vine after vine
Climbing the hillside — that's my book:

Cuttings and berries; death and dung.
Maybe it needs a hundred years
To breed one wine to ravish the tongue.
These are our small beginnings. Cheers!

When both of us are gone to ground
Perhaps our grandson's kids will savour
A deeper red that will astound
Their palates with its baggy flavour.

Meanwhile, we wait, as iced wind knocks
The pane, and pebbles of flung hail
Try to flatten our tough vinestocks —
Hoping, once more, that they will fail.

Scotchman's Hill

THREE CHANTS FOR VOICE AND DIDJERIDU

For Glen Romanis

Rock Lizard

Never move my tail though the sun bang down
Hard on this rock where my back turn brown

You lay your hand over my spine and nothing
Ever flicker even if we both still breathing

Swimming in my rock ten thousand year

If all time only a scratch on a wall
My little clawmarks, nothing at all.

Put your hand right over mine, close eyes.
What size, you Sally? What size, you Jock?

A spear through your heart, and your name in chalk

Turn your eye up to the flame
That burn all time in the ghost-gum tree, and swim

Slow, slow, swim with me into my rock
Into my dream.

Wave Cave

Long one booming under our boots
Big air shudders as it shoots

Bright sea-birds over our heads. All squawk.
Death-birds: red beak, yellow eye, walk

Through the wind and remind us with their sound:
This is the gorge where the sailors drowned.

Under our boots, a huge wave cave
Roof like a crust, waiting like a grave.

If your footing slip, someone reckoned,
Smack black water, takes about a second.

No one who thrashed there ever flushed out.
In water-thunder can't hear him shout.

Keep to the track, son, grip the rail here.
Long way down. Long way down.

Very near

Ceremonial Song For the Cleansing of the Wind

Stand here

Stand here with me

Stand here, out of the way of the wind

Stand here with me in this hollow

Between two mountains

And listen to the wind.

                                  ★

    Stand here, and smell the wind

    What things are carried on the wind

    Do you smell the sulphur-breath,
    Do you smell the death of iron

    And wars, wars

    Where are our brothers, the birds, this morning

    The birds are hiding

                                    ★

        Once we could hear our father's bones
        And the bones sang all the songs we knew
        And the wind was clear
        Stand here, look through this crack
            Look there
        Smudges, black fumes, yellow fumes
          Black poison climbing the air.

            Listen:
            Men behind screens, women, screens
            And their children
            The screens have eaten our memories
            The screens have taken our hearts away
            Men of glass are designing tomorrow's wind

> Tomorrow's disappearing
> So faster, faster
> No sleep, only the screens
> Hurrying. Tomorrow.

Tomorrow's a ghost of iron and dung
Has no secrets, has no tongue

Except the tongue of war and fire
He dies and we die with him

But the screens can't die
They couple with themselves and multiply.

The ghosts of tomorrow are measuring the wind

★

> Stand with me here
> A while
>
> And then go down
>
> When you get there, through the iron air
> Sing for the colors of the wild rosella
> Sing for rain across the town
>
> Sing for the beings in the wind
>
> Sing for those who, in their way,
> Go scrubbing.
>
> > It is time now.
> > Time to be beginning.

FOUR SONGS FOR CHILDREN

It Just Isn't Fair

Because I ate three Eskimos for tea
And seven sausages and half a pie
When Mum came home from work she yelled at me
And both my greedy sisters began to cry:

'He's always doing things like that', they said.
They dragged me to my room and yanked my hair.
My brother poured old dog food on my head.
I tell you, in this house it isn't fair.

Tonight when they're asleep I'll boil the phone.
I'll nail my brother's trousers to the telly —
And in the morning, won't my sisters groan
When all their teddy bears are dressed in jelly.

Oenone's Jingle
    or
Do You Like These Words I Just Learned Them Today?

Daddy, I love you Deliberately,
And Mummy, I love you Refinitely too,
If birds had wings they'd Scriffle past me
And I'd call this house the Potbelly Zoo.

I'd give them names like Doctor's Pointment
Nile Crocodile and Curring Cough;
I'd rub their teeth with Purple Ointment.
That's Twenty Eighteen. That's quite enough!

Where Do Birds Go?

Where do birds when they sleep?
Into the dark, like prayers.
Keep very still and you can hear
Their heart-beats on the stairs.

Where do dogs go when they stop?
They dive into their bones
Forget their tongues, rub off their skins
And doze in the quiet zones;

They wait a thousand thousand years
And then came barking back
As if they never died at all
To pee on my grocery sack.

How man cats patrol the dark?
One great Cat, one only.
With flaming eyes he roams the world —
So sleepless, and so lonely.

I and Franko

How would you like a galoshes breakfast?
No thanks, Franko, I broke my tongue.
Bet you can't catch a passionfruit grapefruit —
Bet you never heard of a — clapperbung.

Listen, Franko — you're always yakking
And yukking, and cracking your toes,
Why don't you wash your head in a bucket —
I don't care if your nose gets froze.

Franko got mad — he stole my bike,
He took Dad's Volvo out of gear.
Dad ran out, shouting *'Spifflicate!'*
Bye, bye Franko — see you next year.

SIX LITTLE SONGS ON TIME

(Bell)
How does the swallow find what skein
Will wind him upward to the tower
Where the big bell in shuttling rain
Hangs un-ringing hour by hour?

(Wheel)
Rising, we strap time on our wrists;
Its tiny wheels divide the day.
We help each other with our masks.
Our masks will tell us what to say.

(Wall)
All day we push this beaded wall
Before us, everywhere we go —
Past towns dissolving under fog
And glacier hollows rammed with snow.

(Fall)
I kicked a rock from the canyon's lip
And watched it plummet down the wall;
And then I let my own life slip
Down with it, down, till dark was all.

(Stall)
A cat's eye glares at me, sharp green,
In cabin-dark, five miles from earth.
My clock has lost its mind, somewhere
Between my ending and my birth.

(Smell)
Wakening early to a whiff
Of flowering thyme, I cannot tell
The dawnlight how your absence grows
Beside me as I breathe that smell.

TWO POPULAR SONGS

It's Over Again

Jenny Holliday's gliding over the river,
She takes the sunlight everywhere she goes,
Past bridges and towers with their juniper flowers
She floats in the wind and warms the morning shadows.

No one's in love with Jenny, she doesn't mind,
She moves in light and shade as she climbs the hill,
Jenny's happy with the way the world's unfolding:
Voices in the grass and wings of the whipporwill.

> *Oh, Jenny, listen to the new day rising*
> *What is it that you've found?*
> *Yellowtails humming in the lilacs:*
> *This is not love, this is love's aftersound.*

Why are you wearing saffron on your shoulders,
Why is your mind as peaceful as the noon?
The winds are bending with you as they take you
Down behind the hill, you'll be returning soon —

But not this way, no never again to your garden,
To your willow plates all sleeping on the shelf,
You'll come back home by another way altogether:
You're breathing again and you're happy with yourself.

> *Oh, Jenny, listen to the new day rising, etc*

No one, Jenny, no one's in love with you,
Your mind is climbing high, it's over again,
You're coming back by another way this evening —
Out to the ocean, rocking on a silver plane.

When you get back the birds will be in mourning;
White everywhere, the river dusted with snow,
When you come back on your silver plane from the ocean
You'll carry the sunlight everywhere you go.

> *Oh, Jenny, listen to the new day rising, etc.*

Hideaway

I climbed through the sharkproof window
And stubbed my toe on the wall,
Said *Sorry* to the floorboards,
They didn't speak at all.

Next I arraigned the cupboard:
Old cocoa and a pear.
I stared at the steel horizon —
What were they doing there?

Hideaway, hideaway,
Burlap curtains, smokey seabirds,
And the wind rising.

More than three years later
The pear had shrunk to a seed
The cocoa chinese lacquer,
The memory of greed.

This room will be my tombstone:
Nothing to think or do.
I climb onto the table.
My mind flaps like a shoe.

Hideaway, hideaway,
Burlap curtains, smokey seabirds,
And the wind rising

SONGS FROM THE DRIFTING HOUSE

For Tommy and Sylvia

A Note from the Bridge

Hard rain clacks around
The drifting house,
We are far out at sea,
We float into the dark
Uneasily.

Frightened bats and insects
Cling to the hull,
The children dream them along;
The wind gets up and barks,
The night's all wrong.

Yet we hold our bearing;
This is the place,
And this the selfsame fever:
Half-way to say it well,
Or say it never.

White Song

A wave of early snow
And rotting leaves
Splatters across the glass.
We're nearing land, watch out
For trees and grass.

What's grass, and what's a tree,
Our daughter asks
Whose eyes are full of snow:
We peer into the white —
Just so, just so.

Bring me a pencil, quickly,
There now, that's a tree,
Trees are like hair, they sprout
And never die. Blankly,
She gazes out.

Antarctica

Somewhere out in the night
A seal coughs loudly:
And suddenly the air
Whitens, the blanket snaps.
Ice in your hair!

A wall of ice towers up:
Quiet, immense —
It nudges the house, a green
Cavern watches us, a green
Cavern looks in.

The Horse Latitudes

Bad-tempered and disgusted
You turn away:
A long day at the wheel,
A stupid, sluggish ground-swell
Bumps the keel.

Disagreeable sound,
A dog being sick.
What are we riding on,
A liquid lettuce-leaf,
An ant's wish-bone?

A ghost comes out, and asks,
Where are we now?
To trouble him, I say:
*No one can tell, the stars
Have blown away.*

In The Painted Ocean

We've eaten well, and drowse
On the warm deck,
The galley's fast improving —
We're almost used to it,
This watery roving.

Sunlight flows around us,
The sea's quite flat,
Once in a while, a fish
Scared by a dog, jumps out
And floats like a dish.

Yesterday when school
Poured out, our keel
Tickling them as we passed,
They plinked about — like kids
On brilliant grass.

Polished ladders gleamed
In the solving light,
A bell rang, the anchor dropped
And all the drifting houses
Suddenly stopped

In a human garden
Where cardinals rinsed
Their throats and bounced in the air.
In the young foliage children
Sang out, and there

The bougainvillia shot
Blossoms of foam
Straight to the sun — and we
Climbed from our heads, and walked
That spuming sea.

JIM BUSBY'S RUNE AT CIDER TIME
for Tim Lloyd

Wind-bitten neighbor's and their wives
Hurry indoors with pails and knives;
The minnjohns multiply with *shunk, shunk*
Of blades on boards. Jim Busby's drunk,
His nose has found a sweating cask
Of last year's best. We pause to ask
If the flavor's satisfactory.
To this he has a brief reply,

There are rare bees in my head.

Empty buckets gape on the ground,
Our arms stiffen as they clank round;
Yellow-tails and vinegar-flies
Dream they're roving in paradise.
Busby snores, his mind becomes
The fruit, the blossom, the apple-gums;
His hands have turned to sleeping wood.
He murmurs in delicious mood

There are rare bees in my head.

His mind's in Devon half the time.
To him the world's a pantomime.
Like smudge-pots on an apple-farm
His mind is smoking — where's the harm?
We break our ass-bones — but what for?
To pay for rags and furniture —
While Busby drifts through his afternoon
With cider, and his little rune

There are rare bees in my head.

from *A TOWN AND COUNTRY SUITE*

for the people of Northfield

The Japanese Windbell's

                jumping again
the leaves ring as well
   there's an angel
asleep
               in the tree
wake up angel
there's work to do
       my hair's walking across the pillow

                          take me by the hair
                               angel
                  angel   pull me
                                            up

                  to the roof of the tree

Hanging Pigeon

Who this hand that choked the bird
Who this arm that jerked the cord
Doused him with light, but stopped his blood?

Pin-feathers warm, he nowhere bruised,
Door nailed shut, room unused
These twenty years. Light blazed,

Came a horrid brief flapping:
Forced the door, found him hung —
Who this hand unwinds the string?

Who breathe on us, who watching?

Warm Day in January

River split, we heard the crack
Run down the valley —

Pools of sunlight gleamed on the track
Wimpled and pearly

Rough icicles dripped from the shack
And glistened queerly;

We snuffed the air for spring — no luck
We snuffed too early —

River will mend its back, dark
Return, and surly

Thick feathered crows
Still breed in the cold shadows.

Blizzard

Hacks at our faces, a low cloud
Spatters our feet with its pale seed
Out on the plain, the dogs
Dive down

By the factory, in a white shock
River's muscles have turned to rock
Out on the plain, the dogs
Dive down

A truck jackknifes, we watch it turn
A brown belly toward the moon
Out on the plain, the dogs
Dive down

Then the snow-wave rams our snout;
The town's buried, moon blacked out
Out on the plain, the dogs
Dive down

This metal womb in which we ride
Might hatch us by the blank road-side
Out on the plain, the dogs
Dive down

Meanwhile, whatever light we know
Comes from ourselves, and the mad snow
Out on the plain, the dogs
Dive down

Bob Broderson's Song of the Wheel

I woke this morning thick in the head
From too much blather and whisky,
I thought my legs were stuck to the bed
And standing would be risky,
I limped downstairs like a clockwork doll
And poked the fire with a fishing-pole
And then my hand picked up this bowl
And I felt young and frisky

I raced to the barn and kicked the switch
And set the pug-mill going.
Some devil or angel grabbed my writs,
I felt my fingers glowing
The tree gave a shout and the dog caught fire
As under my hand the clay climbed higher
And I sang as I sliced it with a wire
Just what can I be doing?

Say what you like, the pot's on the shelf
I don't know why it's there,
I have no way to tell myself
If a pot's as good as a prayer;
I am an ignorant man, like you,
Most of my days I shuffle in glue
But once in a while the wheels runs true
And the spirits of the air
And lust and whisky and summer and cats
And clocks and carrots
And yellow-bellied toads
And horrible weather
Get marvelously
Get marvelously drunk together.

As the April Sunlight

As the April sunlight drew the last
Frost from the ground
We went out puttering and found

By a stone a tiny clump of chives;
As we crushed them between our finger-tips
And tested them with wet lips,

As I watched your slender body moving
This way and that, planning the garden'
I paused, dear lady, asking your pardon,

Because of the fire that climbed in me
To hurry us gently over the hill
And in the young grass take our fill

Of the taste of chives —
And everything besides.

Song of the Central Tree

I tell you, wood
Has always been
My father, and why do you think
The big sky wraps me round.

Woodpecker, woodlouse, raven
These wobbling strings of ants
Ridiculously busy,
These lovers touching in my shade
All belong.

Times I can dress myself
In thinnest glass,
Tread water all day
Or drink
The swiveling light.

All's well with me,
And with my brothers:

I am axle, I am home
And with this excellent hold

I turn the world

THE BIRDS AT PIRRA

*A Performance Suite for Actors,
Dancers and Musicians
1987*

KOOKABURRA KANON

Hey, Jack!

    *Mock a cassowary, jackanapes
      crack a berry (*ka ka*)
    cook a black snake in your
        bomb belly   merry cocky
      mottled rubber robber slapstick (*ka, ka ka*)

                        brown and round
                    as a prowling owl
    (*ka, ka ka*)
              cookie cracker
            macca knocker   occer backer
    snap
                          smack
    snake against the flat rock
    break his back like a footy sock
      and yank him up
          (*ka, ka ka*) flap to the treetop
      slumping all summer
      with your tummy on your bum (*ka ka*)

  healthy as an apricot
   wealthy as a roman slut
    stealthy as a young goanna   track
the misty morning in your yellow eye.

  Hey, Jack!
                mock a cassowary (*kay ko*)
KIKKU!
       kukkabumkoki   kayko
                                  (*ka*)

                              Hey, Jack!

---

* The second voice begins here on the 5th beat (2 beats rest after 'Jack!')

WHITE-FACED HERON

They patched my face with
    bits   of   moonlight
      they stitched me from
        a   thundercloud   so
          perfectly that I can
            balance on every river
           in the wind   in every
          water-eddy   you think
         me delicate   too tall
        to ruin   any   water-
        thing   but look
       more   closely
      the   gods that
     made   me shaped
       a   machine
     can   crack
     with   metal
      beak   the
       tough   clam
        - shell   or
        pluck   the
         quick   skate
          in   one
        s
                             i l
            ver   se-
           cond
           betw   een
             a   fin-
           flash   and
             the   breath
                           of

                                  nothing at all

COCKATOOS

Piss off!

Who needs this racket!
O.K. you're good at changing trees — so what?
Ripped papers
stuck on branches, flapping.

Horrible white witches!
Who needs
your screeches
and your capers.

Stop gobbling seeds
we planted only yesterday.
Cark
someplace else — chew
stringy-bark
go back to the Moog
that made you up.

Go sing in Droog
or Yackanbloodydandah.

In any case,

quit yacketting
and shitting
all over my verandah.

BROLGAS

Fric, fric
  lanky sticks
    claquement de becs
  parmi les roseaux
    et les tiges: Etang
  pullulant de vifs insectes.

Click of a gunlock:

    Battement d'ailes.

       Puis silencieux, effilés,
         frêles.

Ils picorent, ils picotent.

    Legs dry as wicker
      quicker
    than flick of a fish

      bec, bec

         picks him out.

           Then off, on slowly
           waving sails.

Ils se rament tout lentement
autour des marges de l'étang.

        They float.   They rise.

           Pushing the whole world

          down

                down

           and away.

MAGPIES
Gymnorhina
blotched and mottled
elf-bird
hatched and dappled
Gymnorhina tibicen
harlequins with glass eyes glaring evil
double-tinctured, wearing devil
rags across our shoulders
warble on our ocarina
bare-beak
breed by day with white back
breed by night with black back
couple with our cousins
call us *conscpecific* call
us anything at all
and yet remember
don't come near in green September
on your bikes and motor-scooters when
we're multiplying white and black
hide your head-bones
kid, we'll pinch that sweaty cap
right off your head
and make your neck run red
red, red
pied and patched
flecked and splotched
we're out to nettle you
unsettle you
crack your frightened spirit
in the dry creek-bed

and specially when the dusty wind
rolls over on its back
and you feel your brain
turn brown
then black
like us
keep this in the oven of your mind:
we promise you our company
until they coop you up or flush you free
into the wind which owns us
as we own it as we own you and we (every
charred and burning body) drown.

MACROPEUS GIGANTEUS
or THE KANGAROO BIRD

(1)
He carry no wings
or flying things.

This bird
are heavy-furred.

He graze at dusk.
He dream, he twitch an ear.
He hear
every things,
he squirt no musk.

WOLLEN SIE SPAZIEREN GEHEN?

Nein, danke!

I never walks,
I flies.

He take off, bounce,
he thump
his back trunk,
he fly!

He fall again.
He remembering
his daddy.
His daddy jump
Right through the sky.

(2)

(And Now They Graze at the Edge of Time)

                Glide always beneath your meaning

not burning away   not consuming   being ever being

            Our story has no end and no beginning

              We have learned the final skill

    language of leaf and fur   rising bole

              We have learned the oldest thing

                        still

                                        still

            a riffle of fur on the far hill

            a smoke-shadow

                          then nothing

            We are becoming quiet as stones

                Time stuns our paws, time flows
            in shoreless pools around our ears.

    Glide always beneath your drums, your smudged horizons

We disappearing   we, all standing still.

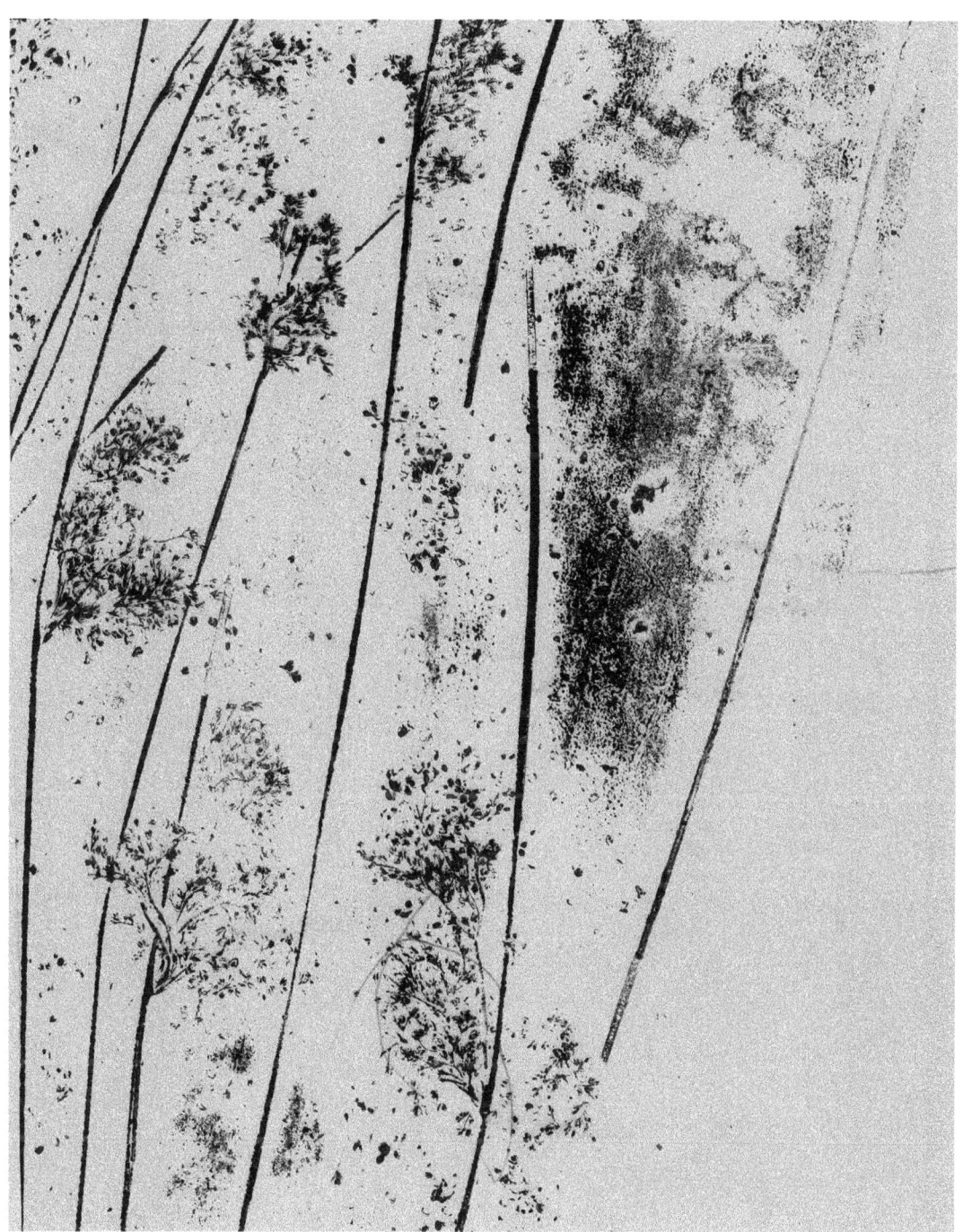

WHITE WAVE
1974–1988

*for my family
in America and Australia*

   1
The same wave bowled me over,
Churned me in the shingle,
A branch of bladderwrack

Hurled shoreward.
Sand in my crotch, I stood up
Rejoicing, the Pacific

Roaring in my ears,
Plunged in again, rammed through
The white wall, and made for

Darker water. Under my legs
The shark cruises by
And then

The huge wave
Trundles me up the shingle;
It was the same wave

Took me, years ago,
And I am home —
The same gull hanging

Motionless above me, pointing east.

          What winds me back
          To this wind-blown bay?

     Sixteen years
     Under fog and snow,
     And in that strangeness
     Found a woman
     In a smoky city.
     Ten years; affection and confusion;
     And found these children

     Who screech
     As the edge of the ocean
     Fizzes over their toes.

What winds me back
Where the wind howls
And still

The granite headland butts its nose
Like a brown bull in the combers?

In my father's house there are many rocks:
Chalcedony and feldspar,
Obsidian and chrysophrase
They speak of the wind and fire
Of the Nullarbor.

Ten million years.

My father gives me rocks.
I turn them quietly in my hand.

Rain on my grandfather's house
Drums on the roof.
I listen to their voices
Winding under the rain.
A hairy hand
Hangs on the wall.
I stare at its eyes.

It's all right, son, it's a tarantula.
They like the rain.

But what if it bites my face!

It's all right, son, sleep now.

Rain on my grandfather's roof,
Brown voices
Drift like smoke under the rain.

Dad, is the spider sleeping?

Yes, son, he's gone away now.

I smell the morning as the house moves out to sea.

Green shadows lengthening on the grass, your body
Tense and hot as you crouch down alone.

Go!

Spikes turning the green world under, smooth river
Taking you straight to the pit, straight home.

Look out, someone crossing!
You veer to the left, keep racing.
Nine inches over. *Foul!*

Come back, come back.
This time drive out faster.
There's a pine-tree by the grandstand. You hit
The board dead centre and climb the tree.

You climb right into the sun.

    2

When the screech-owl speaks
Night gathers about him.
He waits out there, axle of the dark,
Deep in the cottonwood tree.

Moonlight washes the big barn.
It rides on its corners through the night.

There's nothing between ourselves and the moon.

Throw back your head and rinse your mouth with light.

We plunge our heads through a wall of moonlight
Into the barn's black belly, and face
The darkness in ourselves, the hot minds of the ponies
Restless, afraid.

We lunge in with shopping bags;
The red bird splits and
Bright cans bounce on our toes;
Eggs by Jackson Pollock
Wander over the floor.

We lunge in, laughing.
The big dog barks to see such fun.

This is my family,
Their faces shining in the snowlight,

New snow melting in their hair.

★

What's that sound high in the maples?
What's that queer light in the South?

Tree hurls a branch
Straight at the house

And suddenly we're rooted in our bodies.

We run to the cellar
With mattresses, a radio.

Two hours under the boom of surf,
The children hard awake.

At dawn I climb the cellar stair
And still the horizon glares like a wide green eye,

And still the mindless army
Thunders from the South.

A snapped wire whips the ground with orange flames.

Downstairs, I tell them: *it's only*
A passing storm. Sleep now.

We study the joists,
Run fingers over the stones.

We listen,
While the engines churn over us, and spawn.

★

The pointer steadies. Ten below.
Wind ranging in the stubble, scuffing the snow.
No one about. A car drags past
Low, like a singed beetle.
Under the pinewood floor
A water-pump whines at itself —
Then night again, its black mouth,
Its wind-waves. The trees
Walk closer, covering the house.
I've told the children stories again,
Cocooned them as I can
Against this wind that hones its teeth
Like an old unsleeping shark in the boards around us.

★

    If this day were any stiller,
    You'd hear the blackbirds' very thoughts
    As he fixes in his brilliant eye
    The old dog dozing under the sky
    Then, with a flick of his bony head
    He turns to question me instead —
    Who've come alone in the heat of day

Under this hackberry tree, where my life is burning.

I came a stranger to this land.
I let the names fall on my tongue:
Huckleberry bush that crowds the wall
Whose fruit don't please my mouth at all,
These elders where the yellowtails drone
And my daughters, and my son not born —
All strange, all strange as I stand alone

Under this hackberry tree, where my life is burning.

In the old barn I found an emblem
That for a moment cut my breath:
I saw that all these brooding doves
That flap about like madmen's gloves
Like me, are only bits of clay
Who open our wings to slap the day —
And, dreaming on that, I have come alone

Under this hackberry tree, where my life is burning.

They said, You cut the tree, broke faith with friends.
I said, Home of the snail, warm voices in my bones.

They said, Unnatural speech, words without root.
And I replied, I whistled in a mirror, a word nicked me.

They said, This is your home, the sweet taste of returning —
And I, This is my home, always returning:

                         A white wave foaming about my ears.

3

    Three times, full circle,
    Three times over the flashing
    Pewter-skinned Pacific, three times
    Set down on this flat terrain.

    In winter sunlight
    The suburbs poise on the edge of time.

    The houses squat
    Half-lost in shrubs like giant bouillon cubes.

    This is the land where mother rules with quiet power.

    She spins love from her belly in sweet adhesive cables and young men revving their cars down suburban roads frown under the weight that hangs across their chests, and some go mad, some dream of axes, and some hug the sweet cables and come to rest against them like dreaming foetuses, wrinkled and seraphic.

                     This is the river

        always brownswirling

these the willows

                       willow, sing willow

      peewees chortling at the edge of

                                river,

brown river

               thirty-eight years, my father

         swimming in smoke,   *blue hills*

                         burning

Laughing, he grabs my legs, and I
Strike out, and move away. He's followed,
Watching; trips me again, and we wrestle
Fiercely, flop about, and break — to brood

Apart. But when he charges and
Dumps me, I swallow mud
And a white madness flares — and I
Clutch him, pressing his head

Down on the sand in the thrashed water.
He can't wriggle when I squat
Over his chest, and his eyes roll,
Wide with fear and hate

As I force him down. And I will
Kill you, brother — but for this man with hard
Hands wrenching me off, yelling,
Want to drown him, you young bastard?

                                                              Yes, old bastard,

I want

                     to drown him

                             thirty-eight years

          winding me

                                   roots

              brown river

                                                  roots

         of myself

                                  Hawkesbury

Mississippi

        winding me   *hunger*

                                journeys

Melbourne, August 24th

Dear Keith:

Good to see you, if too briefly. We both had our heads down this time. Mine over a microscope. My eyes smart with all the peering. Yeast is unpredictable. You try to outguess it, bring it just a little under control. A form of self-delusion.

Philip tells me you're working on something long. Should I be worried? Not too much terror and gloom, I hope. *The depths are all outside us.* Not sure who said that, even less sure it's true.

Will we see more of you next time around?

Affectionately,
Meg

Over the footy field after the final bell
A swirl of colors as the hordes of Melbourne
Sprint for their gods,
Tug at their jerseys and thwack their buttocks.
And then, by thousands, loose their footballs
In the smoky air. In jeans
And Fletcher Jones and rainbow slacks
They jab at the balls, collide and scramble —
And this is Saturnalia, this is
Why we came. Time for a moment drops its frown.
My brother's face is etched with the years:
The footballs fly.

My thighs pulse, but a cool distance holds me.

And now the gods, like hairy Agamemnons,
Douse themselves in steam,
Sealed off from history and war.

The crowd thins, the colors die.
A late light slants on trees and coffee-stands.

Ten thousand miles from this, dead centre on my wall
I have a photo of a lean man, riding
High on another's shoulders, his hands climbing the sky —
And in that second both men are flying,
Are always flying, the crowd amazed —
As if for a moment they had brushed the sun.

I marvel with what dignity
My people let time wear them down.

They tease each other over breakfast:
Seventy-five years, their hands

Steady, and their minds.
Once more, they laugh their way

Into the fullness of their morning.

A letter from home, a black wind
Roaring in my brain
The music of division.
Four a.m. I am hard awake:
I dreamed the age of ice had come
And wolves fed on wolves in the empty town.

The cigarette tastes of death,
Its mad point follows my hand in the dark
In my father's house there are many rocks.
Ten years. Ten million years.
Ice in the maples:
Wolves feed on wolves in the empty town.

4
They're harvesting. A yellow tractor
Roves in the wheatfield like a giant insect
Coughing blackly, then stops,
Dazed with its own emptiness.

Down here, heads of the elderflowers
Hang in the smoky sun. The day
Burns heavy and green all round, the lilacs
Pulse with their thick power, corn
Stiffens as the sun goes over.

    The time of flutes
    The time of sorrows

          Northfield, Minnesota, September 3rd

    Dear Meg, thank you. Not terror and gloom.
    Dear Meg, thank you, is yeast a metaphor?

I met a woman in a smoky city.
Ten years.
My life, burning —

From that flame two daughters sprang,
Flame in their hair.

They gallop their ponies under the hackberry tree.

Plato said we should stand
Against our pleasures and our pain —
But Plato was weird and had no children.
Gallop your ponies, kids, the new life climbing in you,
Down through the elm-trees latticed
With shadow and sun.

You cannot know the two snakes dancing in your blood,
One pointing down to lust and hunger
The other wriggling up to heaven

And I will be your father as I can
As you hurl yourself toward your certain fall
And I will be your father as I can —

Old busybody, old fuckwit,
                              I'll be your father.

        I marvel with what dignity
        My people let time wear them down.

        My mother comes indoors
        Out of the small rain, carrying flowers.

        And how they care
        For small things, with a proper care —

        The passionfruit vine you pruned last year
        Bore richly, you're proud of its crinkled grenades —

        And who can say, good mother,
        How at the very edge of this

        Your winter, the white
        Camellia that you hold

        So obstinately blooms, and blooms.

6

The screech owl speaks again, and we are night.
The same moon of a year ago
Hangs in the swamp willow.
Its feeble light slides down the wall
Where the footballers reach for heaven.

I am alone with all my years.
They flood back now and I forgive them.
I forgive my mother for choosing me, no evil:
I forgive my father for refusing me
The rites, he could not know:
I forgive my children their small disdain,
It is the shadow-side of loving,
And I forgive all those who looked on me
To bind them and
I set you free.

And if you screech again, dark bird, screech for the amazing fire
That crackles in your feathers, that scorches
The quick snake thrashing in your nails —
Screech for the fear of things lit up in the terrible
Flame of the sun, the night whose rivers
You ride among,
But screech most of all for the marvelous strangeness
Of all creatures exiled under the moon
Who hunger to know themselves
And, damaged, do not wince and, desolate,
Do not break when the stones
Cry out in the midnight wind.

I go through the quiet rooms, remembering.

Have I the courage to accept it all?
The moonlight wanders over the wall.

I am alone, and I am home.

The night is warm, and round.

TRANSLATIONS

THE SQUATTERS
After Rimbaud

Wolf-black, spindle-shanked, green rings round their eyes,
Their knotted fingers clamped onto their bones,
Their skulls humming with a continual snarl —
Like leprous flowers hanging from ancient stones,

They've grafted in their epileptic passion
Their horrid skeletons to the black-spined
Frames of the giant chairs: all day their feet
Through the rachitic rungs stay intertwined

And every day they've felt the heavy sunlight
Percolate through their skins or, as it snowed,
Plaited themselves like this, watching the glass —
Shaking with the pained shaking of a toad.

Their chairs are kind to them: the musty straw
Pressing their angled bones is cracked and dented,
And memories of forgotten sunlight kindle
In swathes of corn where once the grain fermented.

And there they squat, green pianists, chins
Fast on their knees, tapping their quiet fingers:
Their noggins jig in a solemn barcarolle —
A little dance of love that lightly lingers. . .

Good God, don't make them rise! They'll fall apart!
They arch up, like a cat beaten with flails.
Slowly their shoulder plates creak open. *Damn you!*
Their trousers flap about like empty sails.

And then they're off, knocking their polished heads,
Clacking and clacking their gnarled feet, like taws.
The buttons of their suits are fervid eyes
Which hook your gaze down the long corridors.

And then they have an unseen hand, which kills.
On their return their look gives off a poison
Such as they eye of a beaten dog distills;
You break in sweat, as in a ghastly prison.

Seated again, their fists up filthy sleeves,
They brood on those who vilely forced them up
And all day long under their meagre chins
Their bunched tonsils swell with a bitter sap.

And when a bleak fatigue drags at their vizors
They dream upon their arms — of a seat that flares
With sex, benches decked out with petticoats
Dancing around the gloomy secretaires

And flowers of ink that spit out marvellous commas
Cradle them — as the dragonfly is borne
Gently within the calyx of the lily —
And their penis trembles in dry beards of corn.

AFTER PUSHKIN

I loved you once: sometimes my love can still
Warm its ashes with a tiny flame;
But be at peace, I would not have you dwell
On that — no cause for sadness or for blame.

I loved you quietly, expecting nothing;
Now shy, now jealous, racked by fires of hell.
And yet my love was firm, gentle as breathing —
Pray God another love you half so well.

AFTER RILKE

I find you now, in everything that lives,
And all things are my kinsmen: the tiniest grain
In which you sleep, or when your spirit moves
As a huge thunderhead across the plain.

This is your marvelous game, the yielding powers
You breathe through all that's underneath the skies
To swell in roots, vanish in great tree-towers,
Or hang in mist, as when the dead arise.

TRANSATLANTIC VERSIONS
OF RIMBAUD'S 'Ma Bohème'

For Bob Tisdale

So I cleared off, fists in my battered jeans —
Even my jacket seemed a bit unreal:
I needed poetry — and space — needed to feel
The whole thing — needed a girl — exotic scenes. . .

My only T-shirt had a whacking hole:
I was Tom Thumb, harvesting everywhere
Beautiful lines; my pub was near The Bear,
My brilliant stars hummed like a girandole.

I listened to them at a hundred stops
Those fine September nights, feeling the drops
Of dew cold on my face, as I drank the wind —

And, high on poems, at night I'd pull the wires
Of my old boots toward me, like the strings of lyres
And turn it on — one leg pressing my mind.

*

I just goofed off, fists jammed in my levis —
I tell you, man, everything was *unreal!*
Christ, I was full of it — I wanted the whole deal,
You know, the Big Trip — those two week highs.

My only T-shirt had a fantastic rip,
I was Gandalf, grooving everywhere,
Making poems — my pad was near The Bear,
And nights I cooked the stars in a metal cup,

And as I crashed at a million stops
Those great nights in the Fall, I dug the dew-drops
Freezing my hair, and drank the goddam wind —

And, high on poems, tying my fucked up boots
In the dark, the laces made like lutes
As I turned on, one leg breaking my mind.

TWO POEMS BY THEO LEGER

Tomb of an Apostle

They measured the chosen one against the granite slab
Chiselled a word of approbation,
A pagan sun-symbol and an undying name.

Under the heavy stone where love can't die,
In the calm light of the witnessing blood,
His words snuffed out, he dreams of the hot harvest, the victory.

Whoever comes near, proud and alive,
In the reel of lugubrious light can hear
Ripples of mirth under the big stone and the ashes.

A Single Tree

A single tree, a calm muttering giant:
A single archway. Pure night gold. A single
Giving out of a lone bird trilling endlessly
Under night-flames.

An even wind, a wind in the tough leaves
And a man sleeping under the green.

Leave be. Among a thousand images.
Don't worry this dream where your twin image swells
Lips against lips. Leave be.

Leave each fire to its calm. A sharp cry
Touching old suns, dust of a sky
Which burns a little in the tree that dreams you down.

UNDER THE LIME-TREE
After Walther von der Vogelweide

Under the lime-tree near the meadow
My love and I sat down, and there
You might discover where we printed
A light patch in the grass's hair —
Near the forest in a dale
tandaradei
There trilled a single nightingale.

As I came walking to the meadow
I found my love there in his leisure,
And when he welcomed me so warmly,
Mother of Heaven, so sharp a pleasure!
Did he kiss me? Time and again
tandaradei,
Look at my lips, their crimson stain.

Teasingly, quickly, in the meadow
We took our bed in the rich flowers;
A prurient man might shake with laughter
If his steps should follow ours,
And, from the roses, he might say
tandaradei
Just here, or here, out bodies lay.

Anyone telling we had been there
So close, and still, would bring us shame!
No one will guess, though — all that happened
Was just for ourselves and a tiny bird
tandaradei —
Only ourselves and a tiny bird,
Who'll never tell what things *he* heard.

AFTER FRANCIS JAMMES

In a few days it's going to snow.
I remember myself a year ago
Feeling bleak by a deadfall fire.
If anyone had come by then to ask '*What's wrong?*'
I would have told them, '*Nothing, leave me be.*'

I brooded much last year, I remember,
Pent in this room with the grey snow
Winding down. All to no good.
Today, as then, I puff my cherrywood
Pipe with its stem of amber.

My old oak dresser gives off the same fine smell.
And I was a fool because
So little can be changed,
And it's a pose
To shrug away the facts we know so well.

Why do we bother to speak, and brood,
I ask myself. It's odd.
Our feelings have no tongue, yet we understand them,
And the footsteps of a trusted friend
Please us more than a friendly word.

We have given names to all the planets
But do they hear them? And the crass
Figures, proving magnificent comets
Will pass in the dark
Don't make them pass.

And where are all the old regrets
I brooded on? I can hardly recall.
If anyone today came by to ask
What's wrong? I'd only say
'Leave me be, it's nothing. Nothing at all.'

'CORRESPONDANCES'
After Baudelaire

Nature's a temple where each living column
Gives out from time to time commingled cries;
Man walks a grove of symbols, strange and solemn,
Who watch him pass with grave, impartial eyes.

Like long-drawn echoes from the distance, dying
Into a oneness shadowed and profound,
Colors and scents, antiphonally replying,
Vast as darkness, vast as the light, resound.

There are perfumes soft as a dozing child,
Green as a plain, sweet as an oboe's cry;
And others, impure, exultant and wild

Diffusing into their own infinity,
As fragrant amber, musk and frankincense,
Chanting the paen of spirit, and of sense.

FOR HELENE
After Ronsard

When you are old and these words cross your tongue
As you weave by the fire in candle-light,
You will exclaim in wonder and delight,
'Thus Ronsard sang my loveliness when young. . . .'
And then, your servant, dozing from her long
Labors, will stir on hearing you recite
The name 'Ronsard' — and start up in the night
To praise your name in an undying song.

But I'll be under the earth, a boneless ghost,
By hellish myrtle-shade taking my rest.
And you'll be by the fire, bent-up and old

Recalling my love, and your disdain with sorrow.
Live now, I tell you — why wait for tomorrow?
Pluck from today what joy our lives may hold!

STREET CROSSING
After Tomas Tranströmer

Ice-wind slaps my eyes and colored suns
Dance in my tears, now as I cross
The street that's followed me so long, street
Where Greenland summer flames in puddles.

The street's whole power swarms around me —
It wants nothing, remembers nothing.
Under traffic, deep in the ground
The forest waits a thousand years.

I have the idea the street can see me —
Its vision so dim that even the sun's
Only a grey ball of wool in the darkness.
Yet I am shining! The street can see me!

AFTER GERARD DUVAL

It's five long summers since my old grandmother died.
She was some woman that, and I remember well
How we all stood around her grave and cried, and cried,
Some wanting her back, some still angry as hell.

FROM THE JAPANESE

Three Love Poems

Thinking of him again,
I dozed off.
But when he climbed
Into my bed
I made a mistake:
I opened my eyes.

★

The autumn wind
Rasps my body.
And I depend on her
As night
Depends on night.

★

When I think of her
Too much
I put on my bed-clothes
Inside out.

Masters of Haiku

Dozing at noon:
How cool it feels
This sunlit wall against my heels.

                   As it tilted
                   Over water spilled
                   From the camellia's
                   Little bell.

The first freezing rains:
Even the monkeys
Are looking for their coats.

                         River carries
                         Red sun
                         And pours it into the sea.

A shaft of white lightning.

A night heron
Screams at the dark.

                         Autumn winds
                         Have bowled the wild boars

                         Completely out of sight.

Stoke the fire, make it blaze!
Meanwhile, I'll go
Fetch you a gift that will amaze
You: a ball of snow.

                         Too much to drink.

                         Unsleeping, I turn
                         And turn to the edge
                         Of dawn, turn to the sound
                         Of the same snow sifting down.

Last night at this inn,
The harlots and myself
Bush clover and moon:

All sleeping.

                         Remains

                         The summer grass

                         Remains

                         The bright dream of the men-at-arms

                         Remains, remains.

                                  (Matsuo Bashō)

The baby crawls

Butterflies dance on air

The baby crawls.
                (Issa)

                                  A quick gleam —
                                  A trout leaps out of a cloud
                                  In the brilliant stream.

                                          (Onetsura)

A butterfly
Criss
Crosses the

Barley rows

Stitchingthemtogether

        (Sora)

                                    All the snow
                                  I can call my own
                                  Sits on my hat, weighing

                                  Exactly nothing.

                                          (Kikaku)

Spring Poems from the Kokinshu

Early springtime mists
Are rising!

      Somewhere else.

Here, at Yoshino,
Over the mountains of Yoshino
The same snow falls and falls.

                                    (Anon)

Spring light spilling down
And I am blessed until
In the mirror I remark
Snows of myself
Catching in my hair.

                        (Bunya Yashude)

These flowers
Their colors faded
Meaninglessly
I spend my days
And the long rains falling.

                        (Ono no komachi)

Autumn Poems from the Shin Kokinshu

As far as eye can see,
Cherry blossoms and autumn leaves.

      All gone.

   Only a thatched hut, and a bay.
The dark of autumn falling.

                      (Fujiwara Teika)

I gaze all around.

A damp wind off the fields

        Climbs my nostrils.
                      Quail cries.
     Roofs of the village
     Poking through the grass.

After Buson

I step into our bedroom.
Sudden chill:

I have snapped
My dead wife's comb
Under my heel.

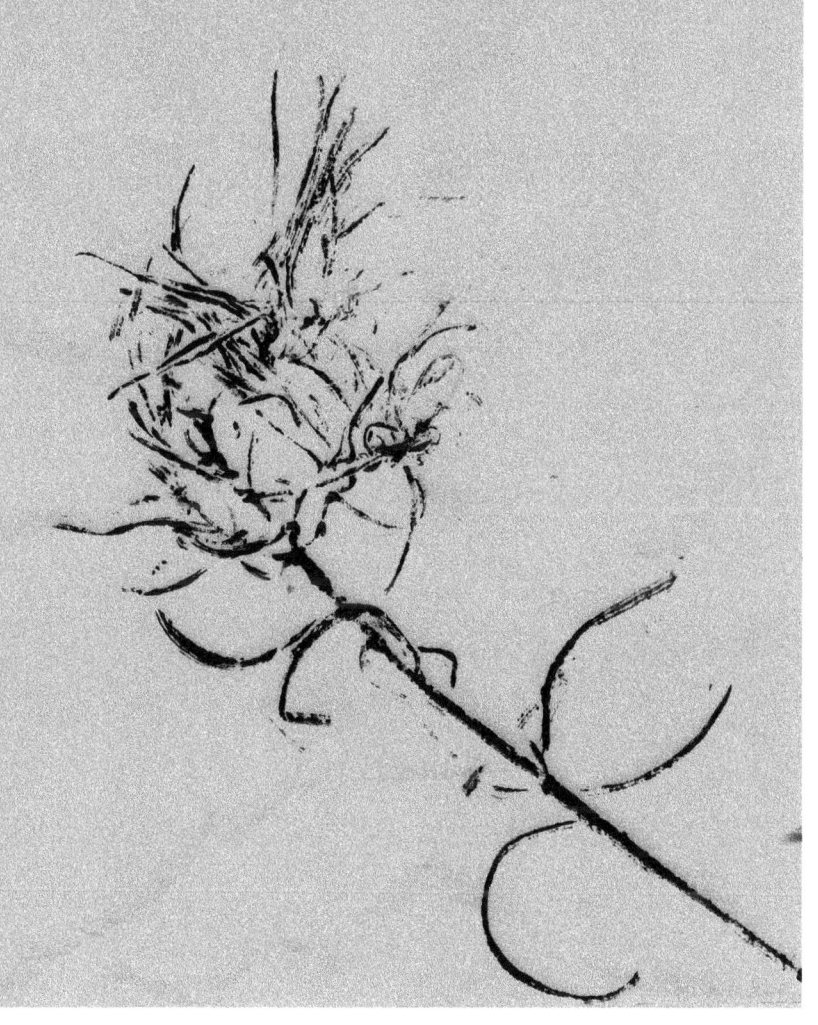

THE COMPLETE BASHO POEMS
1972–1996

THE BASHO POEMS

(1972 & 1981)

for Arthur Gropen,
and for the taxi-driver in Washington, D.C.
who set me laughing

BASHO BESIDE THE MOUNTAIN

There was this message
From K'en Lee's nephew to his father's brother —
Or was it to his father's brother's wife?
Walking beside the mountain,
It occurred to him that he was very small
And somewhat stupid.

               ★

The mountain watched him as he moved:
Slow dot around the giant base.

               ★

A cormorant pierced the smooth
Silk-sheen of water under the mountain.
Basho held his breath, went down with him
Down and down, hunting.
His head began to pound. Red-faced
He suddenly blew it all out.

It's clear I could never be a cormorant, he said.

               ★

Basho flopped down
On a rustic bridge. There were a few
Fat carp dodging among the weeds.
K'en Lee's nephew came by.

Why are you looking down with such intensity —
Do you seek Enlightenment in water?

Neck's tired, Basho said —
Been looking too long
At that bloody mountain.

★

When the harlot confronted Basho
Her jasmine smell almost undid him.
As they undressed he was amazed
At the loveliness of her flanks, the way
Her small breasts bobbled when she laughed.
There are two kinds of harlot, Basho said.

*For the first I have the images of
Spring water pelting over rocks,
A gazelle, a pitcher brimming with honey.
And for the second?*
I find it difficult to think about such people, Basho said.

Then he pinned her to the mountain.
All afternoon.

Afterward it was very simple.

There was the mountain over them, and under them.
There was the bellsound winding over the lake.
And there was jasmine.

★

At about the fortieth twist
In the mountain road
A drunken bandit came at him.
Empty your pockets, he said.

I'm a poet, Basho said.
I live off other people's money.

The bandit lunged at him.

Basho kicked him in the cods. Stalked on.

★

Very well, I'll tell you the Thousand Things, said Basho.

There's bird's wing, the smell of it,
There's the grain of rice that eats you,
Jasmine petals on the executioner's sleeve.
There's knock of water against the keel, the drum at the center.

Certain wines whose bouquets drift into eternity.

There's also rock which is what it is,
The uncommitted bandit who is what he is not
There are dragons that seem mountains
And mountains that seem dragons

And finally, there's the mountain.

That's not a thousand!

Damn right it is, said Basho. Count them again.

★

    Basho's wife said:
                              Where have you been all day?

Pinning a harlot to the mountain.

    You, bag of bones? Your head's so full of dreams
    You couldn't tell a woman from a turkey.

Perhaps it was the jasmine, Basho said.

    But his wife, stirring a pot, didn't hear him.

★

After his descent from the mountain
Basho wrote three poems.
The poems were:

(1) A wind-blasted gull
     Grips the
     Crow's nest:
     The pine bends as the earth
     Hog-rolls.

(2) Moonlight
     Floods my window:
     If a friend looks in tonight
     He'll darken me.

(3) Unbroken light on the lake.
     The cormorant's hunting.
     Heavens, four hours!

Basho read these poems to his wife.

>   *Nothing important*
>   *Can be done*
>   *In seventeen*
>   *Syllables,* she said.

THE THING DIRECT

Reply to the Grammarians

I am a knockabout man of little learning
And almost nothing that will pass for tact.
I like the thing direct: the wolf's wet fang,
Howl of a new-born pig. Appetite. Fact.
The soft *plop* of plum-falls in October
's my kind of music either drunk or sober.
Against the tune that your grammarians sing
I set the landscape of the pigeon's wing.
You who stand back and crookedly explain
Can never quell this hunger in my brain.

Hangover Poem

Must've been the sakë
Immature and sour, that
We drank together:
The mind beneath my hat
Flicks about like a feather,
But cannot find its bird.

Quick Shadow

Strolling in the garden
Comes to spires of lettuce, tall as himself.
A pear-tree snapped by the wind
Sags over the ruined cabbages.
He looks up.
A shadow moves across the mountain
Very quickly.

He shivers,
Trundles his clanking bones indoors.

Sketch for an Aesthetic

If a man is intent on writing,
Basho remarked to a stupid cousin,
He has to study details:
Color of a tiger's belch, the way
Wind wobbles
Before it polishes the pomegranates,
The shape of adverbs in sultry weather;
You also have to understand
The irrationality of water;
How it behaves when you kick it.

When you come to the end of all that
You have to study Man,
The creature whose defining virtue's
To bite the same behind that he tries to sit on.

He Recapitulates/Forecasts the Stages of His Life

Three Minutes Before Birth

Someone poured cold water on my toe.
Insulted, I drew it back, decided
To stay inside.

At Three

A fat fish stood up
Suddenly out of the pool
And flapped himself
Into the sun.

At Fourteen

I begin to understand calligraphy.
From this moment I will be lost.

At Twenty

Blasted with love's excess
I plunge down the mountain
And break my ankle in a ditch.

At Thirty

Whatever engine is running me, it
Missed a stroke. There, on the
Wet roadway, as I looked at the clouds bunched up,
The blank water.

At Forty

If the evil persists at this time
Good may never be at hand.

At Fifty

'Lotus blossoms on smooth water . . .'

At Sixty

'Smooth water . . .'

At Seventy

Lubricious fantasies. The last
Twitch, the first
Twitch.

HIS TRANSMIGRATIONS

Traveling Toward the *Vache Qui Pue* River
or
Basho Attempts to Translate Robert Bly

I am walking very slowly across Minnesota
Inside a car with no engine and no seats.
I have left the seats in a hundred country towns and the
Old squat around on them and dream of onions. In country towns
Sitting down is never the same as standing.
It is dusk but I have forgotten why.
It is also Minnesota, whatever that means.

The moon floats out of the turkey sheds
Dragging the turkeys and their smells with it.
The soybeans are myopic, you can hear them
Sulking and kicking each others' shins.
The lamplight collapses on the grass
Like a spavined frog.

Suddenly the moon flaps past
And smashes itself against the box-elder.
Wearing my bottomless car I slouch over a bridge
And listen with unspeakable sympathy
While two Aquarians try to screw their boat to the river.
I teach them a chorus of the *Vache Qui Pue,* and they
Unscrew the boat. They have never heard
Of Missoula, Montana, where I was happy.

Basho Rejects Hinduism
or
Marshall McLuhan in India

tat tvam asi

tas tati mav

masa tat vit

ma's a tit vat

's i'm a tat vat

(a titva tat, 'm?)

vatsit mata

ta ma, vat's it!

'tat tvam asi' = TAT AM I.

        VAST

        AS T.V.

Happy Day Among the Elephant People

Father, blubber, grease body
Tumbling through the sky.

    'The earth is very peculiar.'

The Sage Who Came by While Basho Was Trying to Restore His Rotten Pear-Tree

I met a man who lived too long;
This was the burden of his song,
Frog's breath, bird-lime, blow on your twisted nail.

I met a man who lived too slow
Seventy years as these things go
His eye turned in and his tooth yellow.

Both long and slow died in a fog
(Two withered tails who'd lost their dog)
One frozen hard beside a log —
One falling far, very rapidly

He Rebukes His Underwear

Fortnightly.
Fought nightly.

Late Breakfast

Bean curd
Bean herd
Been heard
Been turd
Been had
Absurd
Merd

The Crocodiles Who Stayed Too Long

Whatever the fig meant
Was no figment

Whatever the pig lent
Was no pigment payment

Whatever the horses say
There was no horseplay

There were only the spaces, where they'd thrashed about.
The ashes, the bleeding petals, the debris.

Railroad Tanka

I walk the gleaming rails
Ahead of me
Two feet
Above the black horizon
The full moon thunders toward me.

Minnesota Winterdrive

I said to them that this was all the time hardly even moving you have this huge back of the beast I said a million miles in any direction are all the same with the road winding through our eyes and out the back of our heads always I said this is always and no way out of it road road road and any direction of snow snow west and snow snow east where if any god has a hot body he doesn't put his bum down here I said the sun goes five months inside and it stays inside like a cinnamon bear in a hole I said they said why don't you give over you go on too much I said this is a road road oh yes this is a road and what you think you can do about it with all the driving it all just stays the same big fat blackwhite beast like the backside of Betelgeuse all ahead of us and all around and the cold sun crouching in his hole I said they said Jesus belt up get him out of here I said laughing like hell I said you can't even stop this is the road road this is the road.

Basho in Melbourne

I walk through the long suburbs questioning.
No one replies.

SEVEN DREAM POEMS

1

I am in bed with a harlot. We are both covered in sprays of jasmine. There are so many flowers that I cannot find the harlot. An eagle, balanced on the bed-stead points a red beak down at us. I leap up and strangle it and hurl its hot body down into the market place. When I turn round the harlot has gone, though on the heaped flowers she has left a discreet white card. I turn the card over. It is blank on both sides. I stand there shivering, covered with eagle feathers.

2

This time I am inside a jasmine flower. A procession of dead people go by, carrying bootlaces in their right hand. In the other hand they hold flags inscribed with an indecipherable message. They begin to whirl the bootlaces rapidly. They make a noise like a thousand bull-roarers. A dead arm cracks off like a limb from a plaster doll and crashes into the foliage beneath my hideout. I crawl deeper into the flower.

3

The bowl of a brilliantly lacquered lute presses into my belly and begins humming as the wind drives through it. I tune it with my toes. Aha, it sings like a turtle! I rub a leg experimentally across the strings. At first nothing happens, then the hairs get caught and it hurts like hell. I wake my wife up with the shouting.

4

I am rowing a huge black bull across the lake. The bull snuffs the air and wheels forward like a dolphin. I throw back my head, warrior-style and shout *Grah, Grah* into the waves. A storm beats up and we barrel through the black waves singing together. Suddenly there is a haven of sunlight and calm water. My wife has laid out the breakfast in a little bay. There are plates of wild honey and sherbet and a tiny salad of frogs' legs doused in wine. All the plates are floating on lotus leaves. The bull noses among them delicately. Kingfishers flash emerald and scarlet, then dissolve in air. Astride the bull I eat with aristocratic nonchalance. My wife prepares more dishes on the shore.

5

A line of soldiers plunges down the mountain, beating drums, dislodging stones. They break down my door and ram me against the wall.

— Where are all your filthy poems? the leader asks.
— Over there, in that bowl of moonlight.

They smash the bowl and hand the poems round. The soldiers eat them. When they've finished the leader leaps at me and yells into my face WE WANT MORE.

— There aren't any more, you evil-smelling bastard.

I try to kick him but my boot turns into a swan.

6

I write a perfect poem which gathers itself together and walks off the page with a light sneeze. It goes outdoors and squats under the pear-tree. I can hear it talking to the lettuce.

7

A chess-board. Myself against my brother. The kings are taken and only two pieces are left on the board — both white, both pawns. They are on the same file, with one square between them. We shout obscenities about who should move. My wife rushes in and angrily sets the pieces alongside each other. We take each other *en passant*. Then we re-arrange the board. Each player now has half the black and half the white pieces. What delicious complications! We play on serenely.

BASHO DEVISES HIS OBITUARIES

1

The poet Basho is dead. A light has gone out, a gloom has settled on the land. From hundreds of miles the mourners troop toward his tomb, his verses resounding in their hearts. One man, crazed with sorrow, walked off the road and, losing his way in a marsh, drowned himself. There is no end to the sorrow. The governor has sent out functionaries to keep the farmers at their work. But still they leave the fields.

The career and person of Basho are swaddled in enigma. Even those who thought they knew him well find him elusive. On the face of it his life was exemplary. He kept a garden. By habit he rose early, sharpened his pencils and wrote till noon. In the afternoon, fatigued by the labor of composition, he slept. His life was of a simplicity that flowed in everything he touched. Apart from a single indiscretion on the mountain he was faithful, diligent, clear-headed, robust, manly, majestic in purpose, forbidding in repose — and without question he was the best poet in the largest village of the region.

Basho was the ghost in all of you. In a world of complex sewers he asserted the radical normality of trees and pigeons. He understood the quality of metals and the delicate grain of amethyst and agate. The unctuous plumage of the crow, the taste of wild berries, the flesh of women were a language to him. He spent his life trying to translate that language and, once or twice, succeeded. Misunderstood in his life, he now begins his long dialogue with creatures underground. If he can persuade them, maybe they will lift him out so that, once again, he can plunge his head into a spray of blossoms and run his words like fingers through the warm fur of the world.

2
When Basho awoke in his bed
And found he was bloody near dead
He cried out in wonder
'I've made a huge blunder —
I had such a good line in my head.'

He took up his pen in a flash
And slumped at his desk with a crash
When a harlot appeared
And seductively leered.
Her visit quite settled his hash.

3

I knew him quite well in his younger days. Frankly, I thought he was a mean little sod. Stuck-up. Enormous opinion of himself. He hated what our group was doing because most of us were writing better than he was. I liked some of the early things, but after forty he started to write reams of inane pap and all that stuff about pigeons and jasmine. God, who needs it? My own theory is that he was an old lecher posing as a poet — you know, the grave look toward the distant mountains, the sigh of impatience at a question which he thought beneath him. Most of the time he was just too dense to understand.

Most of all he was cruel and ruthless. Do you know that one time up on the mountain he just lashed out and kicked an old farmer in the groin? And then he went around spreading this story about how he was attacked by a bandit. My God, no self-respecting bandit would go near Basho. You could see straightaway that he was penniless. And he'd been wearing the same robe for about forty years, and it stank.

4

All my life I have been afraid of death. I persuaded myself that the thought of death was boring — the hand hesitating over the page, a vision of rats and skulls. Such things keep a man from his business, I thought. To make a small thing well a man needs joy. And who can be joyful when his head is full of death?

And yet, at last, this place is most amusing. They have been eating me for days, and as they eat they carry away the fear. I am becoming part of a vast empire of leaves and minerals. It is a kind of opulent dozing, and I find to my surprise that I am irreducible. Occasionally I hear the sound of people above me, mourning, and one day an old gaffer fell into a marsh, crying out my name. Most amusing. I'll try to reach him.

5
Basho is dead and his ideas.
What can a woman make of that?
Burn his clothes, cover his ears.
Carve on his tomb of modest slate
He was my husband. Fifty years.

AN INTERVIEW WITH BASHO

Basho: "The eye by way of the field-mouse to the comma; the tooth by way of the hiccup to the dream ..."

Interviewer: *What was that?*

B: Nothing. Let's move under the damson tree. It catches the light beautifully about this time. Look at the way the fishboat pushes its arrowhead slowly across the lake. And if you listen carefully you can hear the creak of its rowlocks.

Int: *When did you first start writing?*

B: It's like the pain in your back. It's hard to tell when it got there.

Int: *Can you remember what prompted you to begin?*

B: Pigeons.

Int: *Pigeons?*

B: And cormorants. I've always envied cormorants. Though eating raw fish is hardly my idea of a decent meal. Imagine that frantic wriggling in your throat. Ugh!

Int: *What was it about the pigeons?*

B: The way they flap round like old rags. The angles they make in the wind. There's nothing very beautiful about them. Piglets of the air I call them. But I like the way they launch themselves like a suicide from a ledge then, just when you think they're going to fall to pieces, they suddenly fly.

Int: *What does all that have to do with poetry though?*

B: One line for an image, one image to the line.

Int: *What does that mean?*

B: I'm not sure. I'm working at it.

Int: *Let's go back to the pigeons.*

B: Very well. I'm back.

Int: *I still don't understand.*

B: What don't you understand?

Int: *How they got you started. Pigeons and poetry. I don't get it.*

B: In one language I can think of there are over fifty words for the notion of 'to tremble' — all of them carrying a slight but distinct nuance. Our language is lazy; we have only three or four. Which means that when we come to the flight of the pigeon we are almost completely inarticulate. Yet you can count at least 81 characteristic movements — counter-turn, bank, the wing-tip stand and the side-slip — all kinds of movements. The thing is to find a verb for them and the emotions they awaken. The whole language a kind of verb.

Int: *Have you been exclusively concerned with pigeons all your life?*

B: Heavens, no! That was only a start. Lately I have been studying the rhythm of sea-weed, the texture of black bulls. Lots of things.

Int: *Does the study of linguistics help a writer?*

B: Linguistics talks of phonemes. My basic unit is the croneme.

Int: *The croneme? What kind of a thing is that?*

B: A croneme is the unit of concentration, resonance, opulence and nonsense.

Int: *Can you give an example?*

B: Any word in a good poem is a croneme. One of our modern masters has a narrative which at one point contains the amazing sentence: *So.* In that word he captures very accurately one moment of the pigeon's flight — a tragic moment as it happens: a young boy has just lost his hand and the poet writes, *So.* Very curious. A damned cheek, really.

Int: *But* So *is a phoneme, isn't it?*

B: Maybe. But it's a croneme as well.

Int: *I'm afraid you've lost me.*

B: Don't worry, this is difficult stuff. Break yourself off a plum. They're quite delicious.

Int: *No thanks. Bad digestion. I have to live exclusively off bean curds.*

B: Bean curds! Poor man — even the look of bean curds . . . Well, never mind, let's get on . . .

Int: *Do you think that this is a bad century for a writer to live in?*

B: It certainly is. All centuries are bad. A few years ago in the South someone unearthed a tablet about three thousand years old. On it was an inscription from a father to a son which read, "Take care son, things are going to hell. The end of civilization is near." There have always been gloomy people. We need them for comic relief.

Trouble is that gloominess is nowadays a social obligation. Ask a teacher how his students are doing. "Idiots," he replies. "I work myself sick trying to get the simplest things into them . . . the young are falling apart . . ." And everybody says, *Yes, yes, it's awful isn't it?* Or you go down to the fish market and ask about the catch and the fishmonger says "Almost nothing, the lake's fished out. We're going to starve . . ." And he nods his head and his fat cheeks wobble. It's a kind of convention.

Int: *Do you think the schools are to blame?*

B: Perhaps. But schools have always been bad as well. It's unrealistic to expect them to be otherwise. Mediocre and safe views are the staple of schools. There's been no essential change in that for thousands of years. But there is a difference nowadays. Stupidity used to be accepted as one of the hazards. Now we celebrate it — enthrone it, even. There's such an accumulation of printed rubbish and such an efficient bureaucracy that we can't get out from under it. It's become *de rigueur* to be gloomy and stupid.

Int: *What about the teaching of poetry?*

B: Universal literacy has bred a generation of deaf-mutes. They can *see* all right. But the other senses are asleep. So the whole question of the meaning of a poem has been reduced to one dimension:

> Along the rough rock,
>   an ant staggers under his load:
> He's brought the beetle low, but the
>   huge wing pins him down.

To read that correctly you have to get the accents right. Otherwise you make nonsense of it.

Int: *But you yourself spoke of nonsense as the fourth characteristic of your croneme — now it seems you're reviling it.*

B: Ho, you've pinned me! But watch out, I shall shake you off! The croneme itself is nonsense. I just made it up while we were talking.

Int: *You mean I shouldn't believe in it?*

B: Oh no, you *should* believe in it — it's very serious. There are two kinds of nonsense — the nonsense of poetry and the nonsense of nonsense. "The lamplight falls on all fours on the grass . . ." is probably the first kind — though that's a problematical example, I admit. And if I gave you the 81 poems on the flight of the pigeon you'd have a hell of a time deciding which is which. I did, I can assure you.

Int: *You mean you've written them? I've never seen a copy. Where are they?*

B: I burned them. And the pigeons go on flying.

Int: *How does one tell nonsense from nonsense?*

B: A marvelous question to end with — and look, my wife is bringing us tea. Lacking a harlot there's nothing like jasmine tea, don't you think? And by the way, I should have added a fifth notion to the croneme.

Int: *What's that?*

B: Luck. But there's nowhere to put it. Croneme-*l*. What kind of a word would that make? Let's move out into the sun. Ah, look at that — the steam from our teacups is dissolving the mountain!

Postlude: A Sentimental Elegy

I wish at least that I could die tonight:
Nothing goes right,
All goes right.

I know the central trope reads "born to die."
Pains in my chest
And the crib
Rocking.

Flies bang their
Silly heads.

Who will conciliate?
And what to reconcile?

Sad, yet tipped with humor,
    the moments edge over
    the moments edge
    the moments
    the
    the

from

BASHO'S 81 POEMS ON THE MOODS AND MODES OF THE PIGEON

Bugged by the landlords,
the hard-beaked sparrows,
we take our stand
behind the shit-banks
on the Bank of England.

  g

                                    i
                         y
                                              n
                    f
                      l

                                                  n
                                         o

                              g   s
           p   e
              i

                                         to

                                   in
                                up

                             breaks

                    barn window

                       through the empty

                       smoke pours
                    a stream of whirring

              Dog yaps

These days of wind

I am no better

than a snapped umbrella

stay low, fatty,
you're coming unglued.

roucou-ler

a thousand times

the sound goes round

the barn

rou-cou

rou-ou

rou-cou rou-ler

soon our language will be found

meanwhile

these idiot syllables

will have to do

will do   will do

They're packing horse-dung in a pile.
The horses cannot understand it.

              Your tires
              Kick out pebbles,
              My bomb-body
              Waddles across your
              Raked gravel.
              You say I'm common
              As burdock, crabweed —

              But when this barn's
              Burned and eaten
              Around your absence
              Our wings will make
              Rough music.

Ice in our wings:

our metal bodies

utterly still

the moon

wheeling slowly

around the empty farm

A white cat crunching wing-bones
Eyes me from the granary floor.
Look to your onions, arrogant bum:
Lost in your greedy delirium
With pigeon-lice pricking your skin
You're only a bundle of burning fur —
A complex meal that eats itself,
An ecological sewer.

Dear Cat: I'm heading South.
I've my own lice to lead.

P.S. Die. Immediately.

We bubble like pools of porridge.
Hyde Park Corner.
We've heard it all:

Politics. The art of the
Crunchable.

All the ladies are fat again,
some so pleased with themselves
they bounce their eggs down

                                                                thirty feet.

A startled pigeon
Jumped into my eye, and snapped

The lid.

(sings)

IF I HAD THE WINGS OF A SWALLOW

That way, madness

They've blocked us out of the barn
With chicken-wire and chunks of wood.

Above us the vast October sky.

O the beasts of the earth have their lairs
And the Son of Man has overstuffed chairs
And a wide sweet-smelling bed —
But this night
Under the horrible, thin starlight
The Son of Pigeon
Has nowhere to lay his head.

A sound as real
And round as a pebble,
A big song bouncing off the moon
The rise, the roll, the carol, the creation:
That kind of thing.

Nothing except this dry click in my throat.

> Comes a moment in the affairs of Pigeon
> When almost everything seems dung.
> The reason for the vision's plain:
> Almost everything here *is* dung.

I have been thinking about dogs.
No dog thinks of me.
In this respect I am wasting my life.

                                          Saturday: a blue sound
                                          Full of pigeons

Here's Basho again.
Mooching about in his dirty robe.
What a bore . . .
Fancies he's inventing us
With all those words.
Hey Basho, take that!

It rhymes.

Hard to think
with this idiot moonlight
pouring down:
horses in the yard
can't shake their shadows,
warm engines running,
engines and insects
throbbing under the moon.

Each thing fastened to its shadow.

Most of the statements
my feathers make
stop short.

Like that.

Notes on The Basho Poems

Not only the plan but a good deal of the original imagery was suggested by a student whose haiku lacked a syllable. This book is the missing syllable.

★

The Penguin edition of Basho's diaries, which I have not read, has a number of pages missing.

★

There has been some speculation about the identity of Basho. Some have claimed that he is the re-incarnation of the ancient Japanese poet who is at present living near Dreck, Missouri — which, of course, is nonsense.

★

Basho is a fictional character but his wife is real.

Hackberry Hollow
Northfield, Minnesota
1972 & 1981

WHEN THE IRISH BULLS ROLLED OVER

or

Basho's Brief but Penetrating Study
of
You Know,
the
Whole Schmoo
(1988)

for
Seamus Deane

in honor
of
his escape
to and from Northfield
in the Fall
of 1988

    Stuck.

    Black block. Until.
    Stuck. Word-rock.
    World-rock. Stuck
    Smack-center, white page.
    Until.
    Slow days.
    Snow haze.
    Outside, metal leaves
    On dead wood.
    Enamel sky.
    No green blood in
    Hacked stumps bogged in muck,
    Nor red, in veins
    Pulsing. Head, heart.
    Stuck. Until

Seamus rolls in with his broguish grin
And roguish roiling eye.

Can you play petanques, Seamus?

Petanques? Don't know, never tried.

Plays it all the same, a doozer
First time up and me the loser
All along the gravel track,
He with a street-wise
Gleam in his eyes,
And ram-rod back,
Kissing the piglet on the nose each time and me
As happy as a beetle in a rooster's beak,
Coming unstuck as Irish luck
Leaks out of him, like steam.

Steam us, Seamus, beam on us, and cream us.

Can you play the cello, Seamus, Seamus?

Click, and the big ball sits on the little pig's head.

Cello? Don't know, never tried.

Unstuck. Go home, Seamus, sent to shame us.

(And me with my Celtic ancestors, and all.)

★

    Wine, as I remember.

    Wine: September and November.
    (All October quasi-sober)
    Hammered at the word-bench
    While the grackles gargled and then
    Carked off to the South —
    And there was Seamus doubled over
    (Gloucester at Dover)
    With words, troubled chap, herds
    Of headlong clobber-footed
    Cattle clabbering in his brain
    Mooing for attention and the screen too packed
    For any one mind to ride their backs.

    Seamus, alone,
    Staring at
    Green snow clanking down.

    Stuck.
    White rock.

    Blank horizon rubbing blanker sky.

★

      O Seamus, you will never frame us,
           Said the Irish bull.
We've watched you growing famous, Seamus,
          Seamus, you're a fool;

     Fool for leaving Dublin, Seamus,
        More fool to end up here
    Where everyone's an ignoramus
       And ice grows in your ear.

We fart on exiles when they blame us
      For holding to our ground —
Ones like you that drift off, Seamus:
      You, and Ezra Pound.

At this distance you won't tame us,
     Not from Gitchee Gumee
Pack your bags for Dublin, Seamus —
    Or we'll quatch your quoomie. ★

He thought it was Mnemosyne at first because the edges of the black pool suddenly took form and the still, unthinkable center, and all the time peculiar light from a woman's body, light fuming from the page, and there they were again, the pool, and her flesh blazing from the library book, yes, it must have been because his hand was racing now trying to catch the flicker and the stillness, because a dangerous energy simmered in his fingers, the pages laughing as they grew and rhythms he had carried all his life and never known before, gathering, and the bulls all sleeping now, every single one of them.

It must have been.

Because the clock said midnight in the depth of noon.

The small boy and the serious man together, doubled over, wondering at it all.

*

Brown voice
Warm as tweed.
Word-wise:
Green surprise
Of adjective
That kicks its noun
Upside-down:
The long light
Over stones
Over sour bones
Of history
For a moment clear

This also work
Dignified
As a dug ditch,
And difficult:
Keyboard tuned
To a pitch
Where it almost cracks.

No poetry
That cannot risk
Blackness–
Terminal cell-block:
Novalis, Mandelstam.

Invisible work,
That the rock
In our minds
Might fly.

* Note for Linguists
Quatch and *quoomie* are Australian words of Gaelic origin but unknown meaning.

BASHO PLAYS GOLF
1996

His brother
Calls him. *All right, son,*
You wanna

Play?
                Play what?
(It's early, even
The blue jays

Are snoring.)
Don't give me that, his
Brother snaps.

You left-wing
Intellectuals
Make me sick.

There's ONE game.
Besides, you're too old
For the others.

Myrtle Beach.
Six o'clock. It's three
Hundred bucks.

Be ready.

For nine, or eighteen?
He asks but

The phone's gone
Dead. He turns over,
Tries to sleep,

But his mind
Flares with fantasies:
Tom Lehman

Steering a
Slice around trees, and
Between geese;

Controlled fades;
A long draw that skims
The bunker.

He's flying.
That evening cleans his
Dusty clubs

Practices
In the kitchen — long
Floating drives.

★

Up at four,
Waiting. They set off
In darkness.

Like fishing
He says.
              What?
                  Even
The ravens

Are rubbing
The sleep from their eyes.
Metaphors.

His brother's
Sour this morning.
              Look
This is real

A real ball
A real club. And you.
No room for

Metaphors.
Right, he says, thinking:
The bastard,

I'll show him:
I'll be literal
As all get

-out. *And mean.*
First hole: he tees up
And squints hard.

He can't make
Out the fairway but
Swings, creams it.

Yeah — it's long
And high! His brother
Shakes his head.

Your ball is
Behind you. His tone's
Real neutral.

What?
            Behind
The clubhouse.
                        They find
It, swimming

In the pool
Surrounding the bronze
Statue of

Jack Nicklaus,
Officials swarming
Everywhere

Looking grave,
Snickering. *Two strokes for*
The fountain.

Sir, you must
Tee off again.
                        Thanks.
Myrtle Beach.

Hell with it!
First hole in thirteen.
His brother

Birdies it.
Stay calm, remember
The Buddha.

Next hole. Score:
Sixteen. Course record.
His grandson

Age four, could
Throw the thing up here
In five. Just

Concentrate.
Relax. Swing easy.
Stop thinking.

Concentrate!
By now he's hating
Everyone.

At the ninth
His brother's lead is
Forty-three.

He conducts
A long Socratic
Dialogue

With himself;
Exquisite, balanced.
He recalls

The complete
Metaphysical
Tradition,

East and West:
Madame Blavatsky,
Lotus and

Rose; recalls
The Thousand Things,
Then blurts out

Screw all this!
He kisses all the
Officials

And stalks off.
Even the squirrels
Stop to watch.

I love you.
He waves grandly. *IT'S
A GREAT GAME!*

In the car
His brother's face is
Grooved granite.

*Three hundred
Bucks, and you make a
Fool of me.*

*Three hundred
Bucks, and you wanna
Quit early*

*Like a sick
    Dog.*
    Careful with your
Similes.

*Aw, shut up.
You think too much — or
Not enough.*
                  (pause)
In Japan
It's three thousand.
                  What?
Forget it.

He feels good
Now. He's decided:
Poetry

Not golf. He
Swells with resolve, and
Quietly,

Hums himself
Home with a pleasing
Little rune:

Golf's a dream
Will make a sane man
Very sick;

Metaphors
Might be lethal but
The poison's

Not so quick.

SUBJUNCTIVES
and
Poems Previously Ungathered

REVENGE

My father whacked me with a piece of wood:
Five flashes of pain across my behind
As he hoisted me by the belt. My shirt
Was pocked with mulberry-stains where Ronnie Flood
Had pelted me all afternoon. I was almost seven.
I'd waited in a blank room in the house and pissed
My pants as he called me to the shed.
All week I hated him, remembering
His confusion as he tried to find
A length of pine to get it quickly done.

                If you count them right,
That's more than thirty years ago. Tonight
I walk beside my father and prop his stick
On a rail as we both go down into the water.
One leg's mostly metal, but in the pool
It floats as he swings up on his back,
Recalling the time he barrelled across
The estuary under the screaming of the gulls.

He looks up at the ceiling, smiles
As all the old heaviness drops away.
I walk him round while the weak arm from the stroke
Kneads the water like a feeding fish, and I say,
Put your head back, you're doing fine.
The chlorine water slops about his ears
As the big clock on the wall
Measures out the seconds, watches us all.

I stand on toe-point as we both slide down
Into the darker water. It laps
My chin as I grip his belt and hold my father
Weightless on my finger-tips.

KIDS

Surge like white water round
Our legs and round the kitchen,
They ram slices of apple-pie
Between their teeth, leaving
Bits all over the plate, then bugger off
To shinny up the plum-tree, giggling
So hard they terrify the magpies,
They dunk bread-bits in their Milo,
Sprint through the sprinkler, shouting
Hell with you and hell with you.

Inside again, they scrinch their noses up
And belch, twice, just as Beethoven
Rises to Nirvana. Kids run everywhere
Wearing grape-leaves in their hair, candles
Dripping from their noses.
                              Green sap
Simmering in their bones, kids
Renew us each day with their shrieks
And questions, the way their limp
Limbs hang over the bed-cliffs, dopey
With dawnlight as we lift them
Up to our hearts, smelling of salt
Tidewater flats, and bread-loaves
Hot from the oven.

for Nicholas and Zofia

PLEASURES

When a dancer spins so fast the space around her liquefies;

To get a phrase of Catullus exactly right. You hear his ghost breathing from the page. 'Yes — you've made me new again'.

Delusion and vanity — but sustaining;

When the hot blossoms of the poinciana flare and a glass of water's the only thing you need in the big blue river of the day;

In Tuscany the peasants get tipsy at the end of autumn on last year's wine while new must seethes in the vats. Vinegar-flies drop bacteria bombs through hollows in the foam. You know all that because Vivaldi makes it happen, again and again on the drum-skin of your ear;

When you see your first jacaranda its name is nothing like its flame. As if someone had splattered, all over an elm, small handkerchiefs made of sky;

Today the old German shepherd, being ignorant of death, bumps his tail on the floor and watches me with doleful eyes. *'C'mon, boy. Let's go get 'em'*. He doesn't rise. Dog days. Time for dozing;

Just before sleep the boats of *Then* and *Now* slip from their moorings. Somewhere out there, the currawongs are waiting and I am coming home.

SEVEN THOUGHTS ON POETRY

The best poems walk toward us as lovers do. They don't have to be chased so much as courted. They catch us with a feeling of total recognition and total surprise, as if in the midst of a joyful embrace, a person in love might break off momently and say: 'Where did *you* come from?'

★

To alter the figure: the very best poems we write, maybe four or five in a lifetime, are born with a hot, bloody surge of life, like a new child. They smell of bread fresh from the oven and when you first hug them, they have the tang of a wet dog and the faintest whiff of dung — odors which never quite go away.

★

Apposition is the devil. A lively poem cuts its way into something resistant, making a line that's continually new, as acid does on an etching plate. It doesn't loop back on itself, and rest, but where it burns forward, always forward, at that point there's a feeling of enormous tension, and even of terror.

★

As if an angel with a rough face is pulling you by the hair.

★

We might say the genuinely new poem burns, but what it destroys are most of our previous poems. Nothing personal. It's strange how, in this robust and unexpected company, the weaker poems grow pale and almost completely disappear.

★

Talk of images can miss the point. Almost any writer can make sharp images, but in the best poems the images become something else because they are carried within a dark stream of purpose. We know writers by their purposes. It's not a matter of verbal optics, but of deep plot; of sound, rhythm, the mysteries of tone and tempo — of all these things, and much more, living and breathing together.

★

It's impossible to tell the size of a great poem because when meaning and sound are perfectly fused the substance of the poem has the same valency as that of the world itself, and you can have no proper sense either of its volume or its weight. It's like trying to weigh your own body without a scale. The amount of ink used has nothing to do with a poem's size. Take Buson, who wrote all his poems in 17 Japanese syllables:

> I step into our bedroom.
> Sudden chill:
> I have snapped my dead wife's comb
> Under my heel.

A tiny poem, roughly the size of *Othello*.

PIRRA IN DEEP WINTER

Mist at the end of pencils,
Mist in pillows, fuming in our hair.
Not being mist
We thrust it back, seeking
Clear lines, the cello's
Gutsy vibrato —
Not being mist, not being mist at all.

★

Even the sheep have lost their edges.
Saffron rainlight squeezes the house all day.
Everything here
Hunkers down, rides toward the centre:
An inch, a thousand years.
Soon, in a time beyond trees
They'll dig us up
And marvel at our bones
The quaint design of wrenches, architraves,
Dead rifles.

★

Noon: a river of cooking smells,
Brown voices drifting, birdless air.
Our voices, and our fathers'— who cannot
Shake themselves
Back into their bodies,
But wander everywhere about the house
Like vanless windmills
Raging with desire.

★

Humming the themes of *Was* and
Will Be Soon:
Gong-beat of summer; a clarity
Of wolves in early snow.

★

Fog at the window: Herr Haydn
Brooding at the black piano,
Rose light hesitating
In ancient glass.

★

A ginger tomcat dozes by the fire.
His mother, heavy with others,
Scratches him with her eyes.

A GIFT FOR MY DAUGHTERS

An old train jammed in a box, bogey broken, chimney snapped off. Gift of my daughters from a country auction, in a fat box blazing with tinsel.

They couldn't know what trains had done to me.

At ten, my brother spread his train-bits on the floor. Wrenches, and tiny bolts like the claw-tips of a pigeon. He pieced them together all afternoon, all evening. At midnight the train rocked down the rails and jumped off, churning mad wheels against the hutch. Then Dad got up, red-eyed, and whacked our bums for gouges in the varnish.

And I, who had stood by watching, knew from then that I would never love that train, or any train.

All this unsaid as I undo the tinsel and find my Christmas train.

★

Electric trains thundered past our faces flattening the King's head to creaseless copper. One morning, eager for regicide, I looked up at the white face of the driver ten yards away, his train howling behind him, and I already ruined under the wheels. Some hand lifted me out as the death-wind banged my face. I hunkered down in the bushes, sparks exploding in my sweater.

★

I danced all night on a marble-floor in Majorca. Next day on the northern train for Perpignan, both ankles gargantuan with hot lymph, I propped my legs on an empty seat, whereon a dark-haired woman took them in her cool hands and rubbed them many times, and many times. *It was no dreme, I lay brode wakyng.* Under her hands my life began to flow, the brown fields of Provence and the full vineyards racing by.

And will you thank her, daughters, as we unwrap our gifts, that she took my swollen legs and took my thick heart also, and thank me that, in a station of the metro called la Motte-Picquet-Grenelle, after a time of wordless vacillation, for your sake I turned my back and made this sideways journey into exile?

For, if I did not step down from that train, you were never born.

BEFORE THE BLIZZARD

for Lizzie

Great walls of it, seething in, fast, from Mexico,
Riding over thruways, filling heads with ice.
I have known you nine days, and many seasons,
But none like this, that's why I came
Down a dry road, quickly, the lawns
Green in deep December, to fetch you
From your cool sonata.

The house will rock as tall surf
Thumps the southern wall;
We'll hunker down, thinking of people on the plain,
Wind dragging at their raw-hide roots
And the barn raccoon under the splitting shingles;

And these cats beside us, with sharp eyes,
Their clever bodies folding
Round a warmth that's held four million years
As we stroke them who, more scared
With many fine imaginings than they
As the snow-flak breaks in the hackberries,
Listen and guess, and rub our toes,
Just this side of sleeping.

FALLING

As an awkward kid I prayed beside this bed;
I know each chip and nobble at the head
For sometimes when I knelt here I'd imagine
A wild acanthus or a fruited vine
Might shoot from the wood as I stared and said
God bless us all and make us prosper

And now, a ten-year exile slowly returning
I wake once more to the cold dawnlight burning
The same pepperina, and still the milkman's nag
Clops up the hill and whinnies into his bag.

Not quite what I prayed for, not really
What I meant. I curl against your warm body;
The bed's too narrow and your knees sharp:
Move over, love, or I'll continue falling.

WEDDING SONG

for Karen and Peter

The ball of tumbleweed that danced on the empty air
Told him of human things, but most of all
How love is a standing still, and chance, and care.

He drove by a ruined farmhouse: no one there.
He thought of their work, reduced now to a ball
Of tumbleweed that danced on the empty air.

Then he braked hard and almost hit the deer
That sprang back frightened to the chaparral,
And thought of love, and thought of chance and care.

Oh yes, your door will slam; weighted with care,
You'll think — the house unswept gloom in the hall —
Your days are tumbleweed on empty air,

Then set to work, and the dark day will clear:
It goes like that, the summer and the fall,
For if love's work, it is also chance and care.

Kind chance on your wedding-day has brought us here
To rejoice with you.
                              May your love grow tall,
Not as the tumbleweed in empty air,
But in standing still and flourishing. Take care.

QUESTIONS FOR OENONE

What in your mild latitude
Rubs on wind
Till it shines like scarlet glass?

What has a tide-
less sea inside —
Hangs there, round, and very still?

                    What
               When your teeth cut
                Its thin skin, looses

            Luscious juice that sluices
                Past your uvula, lifts
             Hatches in your nostrils, while

               Flower-scents drift
            Into your head, like smoke of bees,
                Like gratitude?

NOT THINKING NOW

Not thinking now, you step through the pane
Over the ledge, but crack no glass,
Into a world of green
And undulating grass:
The quiet time, just after milking.

Whistling, you walk an empty road.
White houses; smoke rising
High from every hearth.
A sense of breathing everywhere,
And dung-smells and the smell of earth.

Here is a bridge, an aqueduct, a stair,
A donkey-engine with plates of brass;
Five water-mills,
And tools asleep on window sills.
There are no people here, nor anywhere.

Hazy at first, and then more bold
Out of a doorway's sudden gold
You enter the room.
No word wings between us. We stand
Gazing out at the temperate land

In the quiet time, just after milking.

Words for *THE IMMIGRANTS*
A Suite for Voice, Musicians and Dancers

We are further from England than the moon.
From England you can see the moon.

★

    Strange people, legs like sticks,
    Smoke-forms moving among the trees
    Leaving an odor of shell-fish and sweat.

★

How blue the smoke that climbs
From this fire of iron wood
For which we have no name.

★

Today we are splitting cyanide barrels:
    Tiny specks of gold between the staves!
We save, buy seed, plant gardens by the creek.
    We prosper, quietly, we prosper.

★

Hundreds of swagmen passing on bush roads.
Eyes down, we give no greeting.
No work. Then work for nothing. Move on.
Just out of rifle-range, the crows.

★

    To live in this land you must learn
        To dream with it, you must learn the songs.
    These pink men have no dream and their songs
        Dirty the air. Hating themselves
        They take revenge against us and our land.

★

    We shot the last of them this morning.
    They were stubborn to the end.
    We tried to explain, that billabong is ours.
    We really tried:

⋆

    I remember the steppes of Russia as I stamp
    Again this hard salt at the Centre.
    It's all the same. I stamp my boot
    And nothing happens everywhere.

⋆

      These olives, this yellow wine
      Remind us of Crete, but faintly
      As we stretch our mouths against
      Ugly consonants and sliding vowels.

⋆

If you concentrate hard among the stones
Of this cracked chapel where the seawind roams
You can catch the drag and clank of chains.

⋆

      They speak of their Queen, flags flap
            Red and blue from important buildings.
      All day we give our minds and hands
            To arranging fruit in long clean rows.
      What are queens and flags? We cultivate fruit.
           Our daughters will be doctors.

⋆

Here in Footscray
    We carry Mecca in our bones,
Hold to our distinctions.
    There is prayer, and profanation.
There is ritual and slaughter.

    A question of inner strength.
    A question of precision.

⋆

      Australia, drifting northwards
      An inch every million years.
      How quick the currents in our brain
      And on our screens. How ponderous the tides
      Under our shoes.

OTTERS AT BATTLE LAKE

1

The skin of the lake hardens again.
A fat waterbird walks on it,
Looks down at his image, then
Kicks up and flaps a slow curve
Past the Birches Motel and the plastic
Chieftain weeping snow.
Then vanishes among icy pines.

2

At dawn a salmon light
Slicks over the hills, black bones
Of elm and maple
Grip down.
Earth clenches its teeth against the cold.

3

Finns clean their sauna, their blood
Quickening. Their minds go back to
The time of thin porridge, the stench of crowded holds.
Now they swab smoking cedar.
Their Pepsi sign rattles in the wind.
Coins chink in their stiff dungarees.

4

The ghosts are hungry.
The land turns under snow-winds
Like a man who can neither sleep
Nor quite remember.

5

I drive through a stream of spun snow,
The lake flashing on the left,
Hungry with the hunger of a stranger.
A big moon hangs in the windshield.
I want it to drop and wheel along these shallow hills,
Wake the black water, so a field of otters
Dog-heads glistening, may ride toward me
To spank the metal shallows
And slurp the moonlit water
And never care.

BEING HERE

No one
Here in the yellow
Morning clomps
In with clogged
Football boots
The porch door slammed
Shut   no one   only
A blowfly bumps
His head on
Hard blue air
Again, again
Air inside,
Air all round   no wife
With warm hands
Touching
Everywhere
And the corn-husks
Quietly browning.

QUARREL

There's a ghost of bad music
Rampaging through the house.
He makes no sound, hates
All the notes we play;
Cracks our flutes,
Time over time;
Makes my tongue squeak
Incompetent rhymes
In the caverns of my head,
Hugs me like a sour wife in my bed,
Dances when we squabble.

You see that smokeball
Climbing the stair —
That's him, a kind of rickets.
But he's only shaking at the rim;
Inside, his neolithic bones
Are less than air.

That's why the old dalmation
Snoozes there, head flopped
Across the iron dogs of winter.
The ghost has pitched
His voice too low:
He wants the bipeds in the house.
He wants all of us, and now.

And so far he is winning.

GREAT MASTERS

Great masters,
Save Rossini, are
Mostly thin.

Gross people
With too much wind in
Their bowels,

Stretched out on
Deck-chairs, or tanning
On towels

Will never
Forge new songs. That needs
Hunger, this

Side starving.
Save Rossini who,
After years

Of civil
War on himself, and
A dozen

Operas
Lacking overtures
Until those

Last mad nights
When, flushed with claret,
He was dragged

From dinner
To a garret-ful
Of copyists

All shouting
*'Write, Maestro — quickly,
Write it down!'*

Wet pages,
Hurled through the window
And ferried

All over
To mad-eyed fiddlers
And flutists

Wringing hands,
La Gazza Laddra
Winging through

The dark. Then,
In the end, wholly
Discomposed

By too much
Music, he gave up.
It was hell.

Chose instead
The blandishments of
The table;

Chose Paris,
Friends, brilliant evenings.
Then there was

Stevens, who
Strode for hours around
Hartford in

Well-tailored
Pantaloons, new songs
Pouring out

His ears as
He smacked his muzzy
Belly — a

Portly man
Hugely alive, scourge
Of skinny

M.F.A.'s
In sweat-suits, hunting
One lean line.

Had he no
Decency to fake —
If only

For legend's
Sake — just a little
Suffering?

SCRIBBLED IN THE BACK OF THE ORIGIN OF SPECIES AFTER BEING WOKEN FROM AN AFTERNOON NAP

Sunlight strikes across a page of
The Origin of Species. The day,
Suddenly bright and horrible,
Seems to float like a giant zeppelin
With a leak that no one can find.
My daughter sucks a plastic quoit;
She also has a clockwork lamb, whose tail
Spins. The day floats,
Bright, plural and predictable —
You can almost hear the leak if you
Listen closely. Nothing changes.
Evolution's for the birds.

IN SMALL

The yellow tractor
Coughs, and stops against the hill.

Silence everywhere.

It glares at the wheatfield.

⭐

The night you left
I hammered my wedding-ring
Flat.

⭐

His face an old boot
Full of yesterdays

⭐

The word came slowly to his tongue;
The word was *love*.

The curtain shifted,
As if to rebuke him.

⭐

What kind of a father!

She slams the door.
The whole house jangles with guitars.

And still the elm-tree hasn't moved.

⭐

Snap
Of a white *Go* piece
On smooth wood.

Black
Clicks his teeth.

★

    Beethoven booms
    In his lacquered box.

    Outside, wind-chimes
    Wait for wind.

★

Shadow of a broken cross
Riding over tumbled graves.

By candle-light
A silver man
Hanging, head down,
In her lonely valley.

★

    At three a.m.
    Sated lovers turn
    Their backs.

    Fly off,
    Alone.

★

The river's roof
Cracks,
Wobbles downstream

In slow tables.

★

    Two salmon, racing upstream:
    Absolutely still.

★

Fingers in fire
They kick
The man in the snow

Into bits of sparkling air.

A CHAIN OF SAWS

A costive artist is a howling contradiction

The pedant trembles with fear at the thought of possible mistakes.
The artists gathers up his mistakes and hammers them into the pavement of the Great City.

Clear water flowing evenly off the rock-ledge. Sunlight bursting in it.
The painting going well.

Irony is fear's dishonest brother.

From Srinigar to Madras, the crows, the crows.
They squat on the ground like bloated commas.

If your neighbor is committed to killing himself, help him.
If your neighbor is committed to killing you, lend him a wolf.

Two artist arguing. An impossibility.
Two artists not arguing. An impossibility.

Keats is not a better poet than Whitman. They are absolutely equal.
Just as an alligator is the equal of an avocado.

The man of power, sleepless at dawn, rocks in his loneliness.
An empty clothes-hanger in an empty wardrobe.

The painter moves quietly, concentratedly, toward the clean canvas.
The crow whets his beak.

A poem is a strategy for encompassing a situation (Burke)
A situation is a strategy for encompassing a Burke (poem)
A Burke is a poem for encompassing a strategy (situation)

(Burke)

ELEGY FOR A STARING BOY

If I were wind
I'd crack this box you call a house
And hurl the roof away
Where the young boy squats
Flattening his mind against a screen
All night, all day
Destroying images, Jack and the Beanstalk
Having gone, and scour
The wreck with rain, rolling
Plastic tractors and smashed toys
Downstream to the Gulf, yes, make it
An honest ruin full of rats and lightning
In this sour district, where cops lever
Black women against their cars
And lift their skirts
And press them till they scream,
Where no one saw the fledgeling kestrel
Tumble from the maple-tree
And no one asks the boy
Why are you growing down like this
To a half-man smoking under the stars?

We pensioners are irrelevant, we read
Dusty books and shuffle about
Remembering magpies
Fluffing their wings in a sun-shower
While moonless alleys fill with the boom of neons
And the screech of electronic hawks
On channel 269.

APPROACHING MINNEAPOLIS BY CAR

Out there, skinny pheasants rattle the cornstalks
And further out, the dogs climb down to sleep.
It's getting cold, the stars harden —
And under our wheels the burden of strange machines.

Neons flare then drift back in darkness.
Over the city, the clouds are singed
Unnatural white, unnatural orange.
The skiers crouch, and hack the luminous hill.

RED FOX IN WINTER

The edge of the city turns over in sleep.
Hulks of cars budge and resettle, an undulation
As of shells in deep water.

Over America
The clouds accelerate, and spill
Black seeds along the highways.

The red fox curls in himself, waiting.

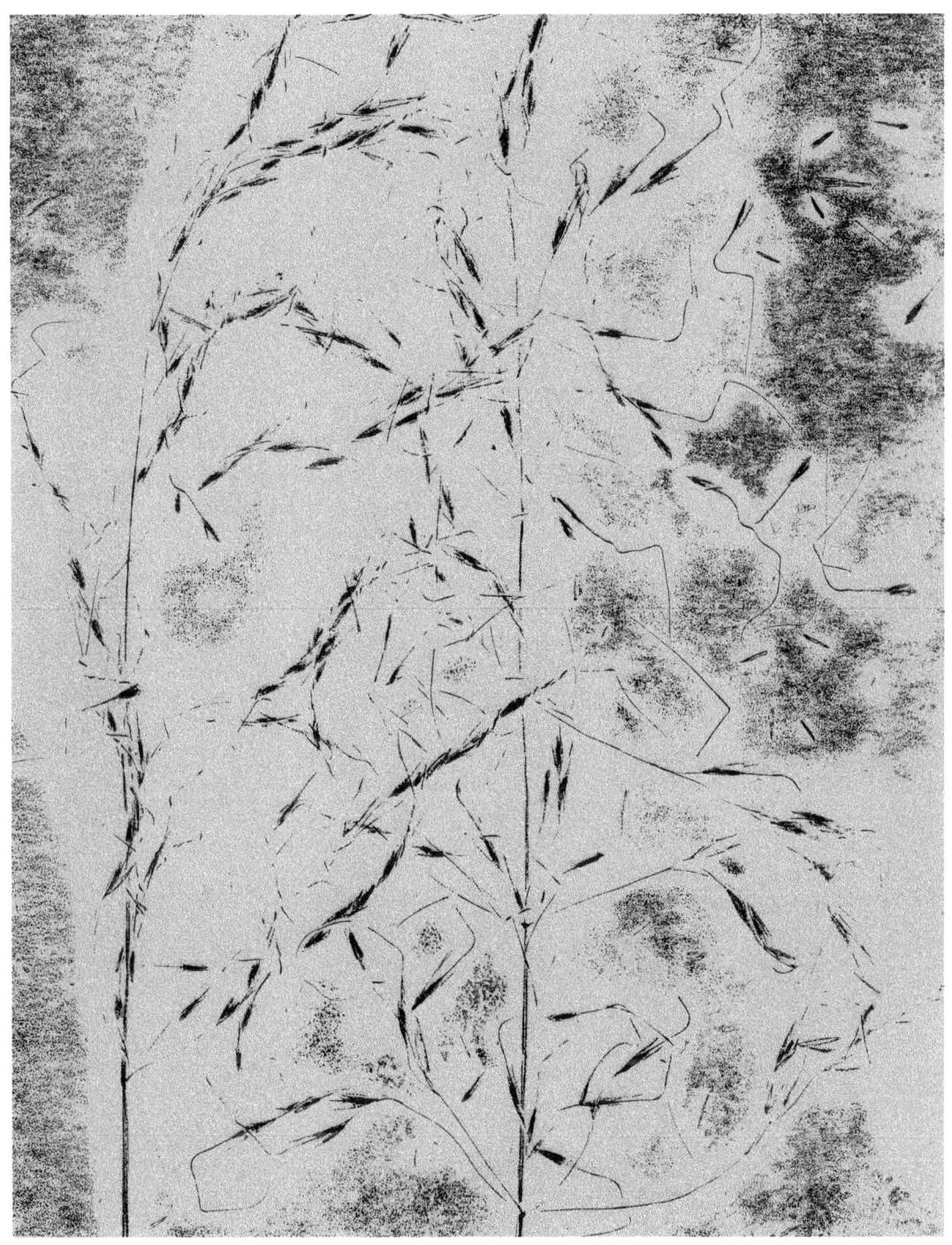

SNAIL-TRACKS
New Poems 1993-2002

There is another world;
It is beyond this one.

There is another world;
It is within this one.

There is another world;
It is the same as this one.

THANK YOU, PYTHAGORAS

This little
Wavering dance: two
Threes and five

Fits me well;
It keeps my flatfoot
Wits jumping;

It can flick
Fast as a tomtit's
Tail — or move

Extremely
Slow, like mauve seaweed
Pulsing in

A green sea.
Here, one small word can
Swell, to a

Landscape wide
As Minnesota,
Or even

Wider — say
To the blind dark of
Milton's Hell.

A certain
Mathematical
Imp or spell

Hides in it.
Most anything goes
Within its

Free confines:
Pop, be-bop, jumped up
Reggae bump

Bums against
Karlheinz Stockhausen
And Berio.

If Dante,
Instead of terza
Rima, had

Found this thinned
Down version, he would
Have wet his

Pants. Just think
Of the eyes saved and the
Printer's ink.

SERIOUSLY

Soon we'll be
Gone from here, leaving
No traces

Save in our
Surest mimics — our
Kids' faces;

Shelf-loads of
Books, and some verses
That might stand

Fifty years
From now, and still sing.
Maybe not;

The wasted
Words will rot, with my
Snow-blasted

Trees, which are
Not mine anyway
I'm afraid.

Strange: I'm sure
I hurried back here
This time for

Something more.
But if you asked, What
Was it? I'd

Say, *That's hard*.
I'm like a man who's
Left something

Important
Indoors, but stops to
Watch grackles

Jabbering
On the lawn. I guess
The grackles

Beguiled me —
Though I would insist
I'm looking

Every day
For that serious thing —
But not, it

Now seems (and
Might well be) quite so
Seriously.

HANDS

Here you are
Again, blunt spiders,
Both of you

Three legs short:
You scutter up smooth
Wood; you choke

Mop-handles.
Smart-asses, always
Acting for

Yourselves! You
Clam up, rub bellies
Together

In sharp wind.
Why are you hiding there
In hairy

Darkness on
My pillow? I don't
Know you. Where

Are your eyes?

CAROLINE

The night you
Took our breath away
When you turned

Your dark hair
Lustrous as a mink's
Fur, I swear

I never
Dreamed black could be so
Sudden and

So lively:
A loveliness like
Snow, or fire.

Two weeks on,
Remembering you,
I'm wondering:

That lioness
Close by your tent who
Startled you

When she snarled
At the stars, so close
You could hear

Her breathing —
Surely, watching you
Next day in

Full light, in
Some deserted kraal,
Gunless and

Unafraid,
Even she, in pained
Envy, would,

On seeing
The beauty of your
Brilliant mane,

Have howled, with
An almost human
Sound, before

She rose up
And, remembering
Her hunger,

Sprang.

EVEN STEVENS

Kelpies dodge
Between their pup-yaps
And last bones

But even
Last bones aren't final:
Sun-whacked, they

Break up and
Blossom in wheat or
Thistle-spikes.

This is our
Damnation: never
Arriving;

Also our
Only paradise —
As Stevens

Reminds us
Paradoxically,
With changing

Things that stay
There on the page — e.
g. *blackbirds*.

COUSIN JOCK

His home a
Musty warehouse full
Of broken

Chairs and clocks;
Living between ten
Chewed-up jokes;

Lungs blasted
With nicotine, heart-
muscle fat;

An odor
Of old peanut-shells
And ashes,

Smokes all day
And much of the night.
The kitchen's

Oddly neat;
Works there without aim —
A furious

Emptiness.
But still the conscience
Of our clan:

Family first,
Son, he reminds
Me. He's right,

Of course. Takes
Obscure cousins and
Their sick cats

All over;
Call doctors; buries
Everyone.

Introduced
To the Queen, he said,
'Nice titfer!'

Balmoral's
Nice too — so please don't
Mansion it.'

His story,
And probably true
(Do I wince

In pain or
Envy?) Ruins all talk
With word-farts;

Laughs louder
Than 747's
Taking off.

Still caring
For all of us — and
Here I am

Once again
Running away from
His huge voice,

Hurrying
To America,
Feeling mean.

JUSTICE BARRIE AND HIS MISTRESS

Two Telegrams

*Buy gloves, and
Silk panties.*

Right. Send
Finger-size.

(Dimensions
Of your bum I know
Precisely.)

(Melbourne-Paris, 1911)

AT SUPPER, NOT WHERE HE EATS
For Arthur Gropen and Trish Lewis

We are his
Special guests from the
U.S. so

Akima
Calls for his special
Fish dish. We

Wait. Hours.
Round midnight, dressed with
Sea-grass, shells

And lemons,
Most royally, the
Fish swims in.

He is sliced
Delicately from
Gill to tail.

Someone says,
'Look, he's still breathing
He's alive!'

And the fish
Watching us all with
Leaden eyes.

Akima,
Showing off, rubs his
Hand across

The fish's
Jaw. At which he leaps
From the plate

And bites him
Hard. Akima jumps
Back and (most

Unlike his
Kin, the samurai)
Starts yowling

Trying to
Shake the thing off his
Hooked fingers

Showering
Fish-bits and his own
Blood over

The table.
This ceremony
Gains our full

Attention,
While serving-women
Hurry off

To fetch salves,
Long bandages — and
A new fish

But no — they've
Re-assembled the
Ruined one

And he's still
Half-alive, his tired
Eyes glazing.

Akima
Raises his wounded
Sword-hand, as

If the fish
Should honor him. He
Leans back, a

Full fathom
Length, and studies him.
No one stirs.

Then, gaining
Courage, we close in
And eat him.

LEAVINGS

For M.W.

Margaret,
Are you still grieving
All for that

Lanky dick
Who bled you white, then
Let you go?

He was no
Golden grove for you
To dance in

But, in short,
A cunning snout. Look —
Out there, in

Your garden
Last year's trees are still
Leaving, and

Not leaving.
But what's left, you ask,
After all

This? Days and
Years. Wind against your
Handsome face,

Heart bumping,
The certainty of
Fall. Meanwhile,

Rejoice in
Being thus relieved.
Such bitter

Readings as
We made tonight are
Only for

Old lovers
In their cups. *You wash,
I'll dry. Let's*

Flush them out.

CATULLUS IN A DATSUN

When I'm back
We'll come together
Joyfully,

Then worry;
And part again;
Join again.

Catullus
Had this sickness, and
Perished young;

All those years
Muttering: *Lesbia,*
Fuckbird, whore

Give over!
Hot poems, exuding
From his tongue.

She, tupped by
Almost everyone
Of note, and

Some others
(Even her brothers)
Wheedled her

Wasting years
Through brothels, her mind
Shot. And what

Of us? I've
Journeyed ten thousand
Miles, trying

To come clear;
Driven, driven and am
Stuck. This is

Hell. White day
Vibrates, this treeless
Road's too long;

Your perfume
Still invades the air.
I did not

Choose this way
To scuttle us nor,
Least of all,

Confuse you.
Excuse my failure
But it's clear

Australia's
Not quite big enough
To lose you.

T-SHIRT POEMS: *The Seven Seasons*

Morning flares
In the curtains. Quick,
Wake up, take

Me now. I
Will be ravished in
Lilac-light!

                          Flies doze on
                    A brown rose, dreaming
                            Of nectar.

                            Crystals in
                  Their huge eyes glow like
                        Church windows.

Green burns down
In urns of burnished
Umber gold

   As if a
Sultan's roof drowned in
  Copper-flames.

                        A ketch heels
                      Over in white sea.
                      The boom strikes

                    Out. Spill, sail,
                    Ladle the air, then
                      Shake yourself.

                      Faster than
                    Shot-pellet, or a
                    Sprung slingshot

                      A sharp bird
                    Stabs an apricot.
                    The rot starts.

      Spiders spin
Frail bridges that span
      Black furrows

     Where empty
Cornstalks crack and a
   White wind blows.

                         Icicle?
                  Fang of a god? Stop
                    Thinking! Snap

                      It off, fast!
              Feed it to the stove's
                    Blazing mouth.

WIMMERA SNAKE-TIME

Drove up here
Forty years ago;
Remember

How, at dawn
In the smoky light
I saw the

Tiger-snake,
Stretched out across the
Tar, rising

At me, fast:
Stood up, terrified,
Braking hard:

If my wheels
Flick him up, over
My back, he'll

Bite my neck!
Too late! My tires crack
His back-bone,

And I wait.
Nothing. Already
Many wheels

Had ruined him:
His bright striations
All ripped and

Bloodied, he
Lay there, receding
In my mind.

And was it
Five miles, or ten bronze
Summer's back

I passed a
Struck roo dreaming on
His side —

A big grey
Still woven in his
Gauze of flies?

I pull up.
I look all around.
Nothing moves.

Grass whitens
In the migraine heat,
The same dead

Ghost-gum on
The same singed hill cracks
Without sound.

You have been
To America,
Born daughters

And come home
To this heat where you
Own nothing;

Drive on. Time
Is the queerest place
We live in.

LIONS, etc

I hope death
Might cut me short as,
Whistling, I

Flip an egg
Sunny-side down, or
Prise the cork

From a dusty
Rutherglen: Quick,
Just like that!

Seabirds drop,
After all, in flight.
Or — if it

Must be slow —
As a lion, jaw-bone
Cracked by a

Zebra's hoof,
Squatting by a pool
Three whole days

Never thinking
Of sorrow. For him
It's a time

For changing
Kingdoms. Our kind are
Obstinate:

We hang on
Hard, wishing for the
Reprieve of,

Please, one more
Birthday, as if to
Fool death with

Candle-light
Faustian bargains,
Dreams. Listen,

Good daughters,
Should my luck fail and
My brain-pan

Go fut, should
Fresh words stop tumbling
From my tongue,

Should I stare
Nightlong, daylong at
The ceiling,

Kept pulsing
Only by tubes and
Dials — please

As I would
For you — pull the plug,
Send me on

Where I can
Go on changing. There's
A time — let

It be clean
And sharp — for grieving.
Then rejoice;

I have known
Riches beyond my
Deserving.

Remember
The dead, though their tongues
Are extinct,

Will insist
On scattering their
Dry advice.

You must blow
Hot breath into the
Sockets of

Their mouths, tread
With rough boots over
Their bones and

Stubbornly
Decline our frequent
Offers to

Bring you down.

CODICIL

When I'm ash
Sift me in equal
Measures, then

Scatter half
Of me on Wild Dog
Creek where it

Meets the sea.
Strew on Lake Pepin
What remains.

I shall be
Home there, on waters
I have loved.

Fling me wide,
With the best music
You can find.

Canberra, June 22, 2002

MOTHER AND DAD AT NINETY-THREE

My father's
Winding down, who once
Lifted me

High, to watch
A scruffy ape scratch
His fleas, and

Higher for
Great music, and more,
Much more. Please

Forgive me
Dad, I would lift you
In your turn

But the zoo's
Are shut, and my arms
Fail me. So

I stand still.
He smiles, turns his head.
It's okay

*Son, I know,
I understand.* I feel
Him sliding

Away. Then
He starts up: *Listen,
I've designed*

*A plane with
Eight wings. It will save
The whole town!*

This with such
Passion for a mad
Second I

Believe him.
Words from a country
In his brain

That's always
Young. Now he falls back
And dreams. He

Smiles, and schemes.
★
What to say
Of my old mother,
Jess, who can

Turn a heel
Fast, without looking
And still scan

A mis-hit
Backhand? She can hear
Owls thinking,

Cut whopping
Turnips right through, and skin
Eels, but not

Those that Dad
Goes hunting each night
In his head;

The black ones
That make you vomit
When half-cooked.

No morning
In this century
Has held her

Down. Her eyes
Sparkle as she knits,
Correcting

All errors:
Of facts, dates — and our
Atrocious

Grammar.

PROFONDEURS AT 2 a.m.

This late jazz
Without direction
Sours the mind.

In the night
Men kill each other
Endlessly.

The music
Goes on: Angola,
Rwanda,

And each night
You take your toothbrush
From the wall

And each night
Dig your little death
Like a blind

Cistercian.
Your children orphaned
In a far

City. Dig.
One more day, one less.
These ghosts, these

Shelves and books;
Discarded papers.
Solitude.

SNAIL
-TRACKS

      Your dawn-call
      Startled me. And then
      I lay still,

      Wondering:
      Such hunger at ten
      Thousand miles!

                                    Jealousy
                                    Has so fine an ear
                                    It can catch

                                    The creak of
                                    Bed-springs, clear across
                                    Five counties.

                Love occurs
                Variously. Bears
                Rub their fur

                Backwards, till
                Sparks fly. Then they romp
                And tumble.

          Ezra Pound
          Taught us to think hard
          About sound —

          The shuttle
          Of live syllables:
          That was all.

When I'm gone
Think of me when snail
-tracks appear:

I have tried
These years to make such
Frail silver.

NOTES ON THE POEMS

WORDS AGAINST WAR

In My Freshman Year, p. 33
Harold Henderson, Paul Smith and David Loy, three Carleton freshmen, as a protest against America's military actions in Vietnam, burnt their draft cards before a large crowd in Great Hall in September 1968. History has fully vindicated the stance that those students, and many like them throughout the country, took at that time.

Legs, p. 34
At a trial New York after the Gulf War fourteen international judges, using the same legal arguments as in the trial of the Nazi war criminals at Nurenberg, indicted President Bush, Defense Secretary Richard Cheney and General Collin Powell for crimes against humanity. Few people know about that trial. It was outlawed and completely boycotted by the media. Ramsey Clark's book, *The Fire This Time,* gives a full account.

Shakespeare's Prince Hal (who later becomes Henry V), in his coldness, intelligence and opportunism, seems a very 'modern' politician. I learned after I wrote this poem that the super-computer used in the film *2001: A Space Odyssey* was also nick-named Hal.

General, p. 35
The poem is not primarily a castigation of General Schwarzkopf. It is a condemnation of the whole Empire that produced him and vindicated what he achieved. Nor is it our leaders who are uniquely to blame. We elected them.

Field-Notes for the War Against England, p. 37
People often remark that Australians and Americans are alike. There are, in fact, many subtle differences, but there is one absolutely startling one, which is very often overlooked, especially in Australia: America, in the 18th century declared war on England and won that war. That difference accounts for a great deal.

Robert Hughes' excellent book, *The Fatal Shore,* gives a very different view of the early colonial period in Australia either from the one we learned in school or the one that most people in Britain and America have come to believe.

An experiment, devised by the British Army American Armies in Australia, used a number Australian 'volunteers' in a 'secret and dangerous' mission. A dozen or so soldiers were pushed to the point of exhaustion over a long assault course in the tropics, sealed up immediately in a Quonset hut and sprayed heavily with mustard-gas. After a brief interval this process was repeated. The aim was to see if heavy sweating increased the destructive effects of the gas. Predictably, it did. The ruins of some of those men, now very old, are still walking about in various parts of Australia.

The Reverend Samuel Marsden (1764–1838), a particularly unsavoury colonial missionary, took a pathological pleasure in watching Irish convicts being flogged.

PORTRAITS, MASKS & MONOLOGUES

Olof Andersson's Rune, p. 128
Robert Bly once told me that it was a custom in ancient Scandinavia for a man to write a secret song about his life, place it in a bottle or jar, and bury it somewhere in the root of the house, or under a tree. It was to be read only after the writer's death. It was believed that if the song were discovered prematurely its owner would die.

ORCHARD POEMS

A Burning of Applewood, p. 143
I had Lorenzetti's **The Idea of Good Government in the Country** in mind when I wrote this poem. I had seen it in Italy but couldn't remember the name of the artist. In the heat of composition I used the fictive name Ludovico, partly because of the rhythm and, in the end, decided to keep it.

Ballad, p. 147
Michel Dennis Browne once sketched for me outline of a narrative poem by a writer whom (as I understood) he couldn't trace. The ghost of that poem haunted me for months. Its last line 'And then they opened the door and we were angels' (which was the only line he gave me verbatim), still seems to me on of the most poignant and memorable lines in modern poetry. One day, using that shadow poem as prompt, in a burst of terror I wrote my own version, using for setting my cousin's 'block' on the River Murray near Waikerie, South Australia. Later I discovered that the original poem was by the poet Roland Flint. I wrote him, immediately, telling

what I had done. I explained that I would always acknowledge his poem when I read or published my own version. I also asked for a copy of his poem but, to this day, I have not received it.

The mindless technology which produced refrigerator doors that could not be opened from inside, and caused the death of many children, is now, mercifully, outlawed. The speaker of here is a boy of about fourteen.

THE BIRDS AT PIRRA, p. 199

Kookaburra Kanon. The kookaburra (*Daecolo novaeguinae*) is found in almost all wooded areas in the East of Australia and also on the southern part of the West Coast. A species of kingfisher, it is sometimes called the Laughing Jackass because of its rather staccato cackle. The kookaburra is a skilled hunter of insects, crabs, fish — and even chickens and large snakes.

The **White-faced Heron**, (*Ardea novaehollandiae*) sometimes called the Blue Crane or White-fronted Heron, can be found in most of Australia's rapidly shrinking wetlands and swamps. It eats yabbies (crawdads), insects, freshwater snails and frogs.

Cockatoos (from the Dutch *kaketoe*, Malay *kakatua*). Descending in raucous squadrons, cockatoos have been known to eat parts of the sidings of weatherboard houses.

Macropeus Giganteus: not a bird. We wanted to add to the legends. The second poem is an attempt to capture some of the delicate and mysterious qualities of this tough marsupial which has been at home on its huge island for millions of years.

Australian **Magpies,** *Gymnorhina tibicen,* are no relation to their English namesakes. They can be very virulent neck- and skull-peckers in the breeding season but they have a beguiling warble, especially in the early morning.

Sometimes called the *Native Companion*, **Brolgas** (*Grus Rubicunda*) are versatile dancers, even when not courting. Their call is a chesty trumpeting, their flight langorous and easy.

INDEX OF TITLES

(Titles of individual poems and sequences are shown in roman type. Titles of poems within sequences are shown in italics.)

After Buson, 241
After Francis Jammes, 234
After Gerard Duval, 236
After Pushkin, 230
After Rilke, 230
After Tomas Tranströmer, 236
Angle, 18
Antarctica, 188
Approaching Minneapolis by Car, 325
As the April Sunlight, 194
At Ouray, 17
At Supper, Not Where he Eats, 339
At the River, 66
At the Edge of Winter, 129
Australian Tongues, 131
Autumn Afternoon, with Birds, 70
Autumn Poems from the Shin Kokinshu, 240
Ballad, 147
Barracoutta Fisherman: Tasmania, 131
Basho Beside the Mountain, 249
Basho Devises His Obituaries, 262
Basho in Melbourne, 259
Basho Plays Golf, 293
Basho Rejects Hinduism, 257
Battersea: Just before Dark, 69
Bees, The, 46
Before the Blizzard, 311
Being Here, 317
Birds at Pirra, The, 199
Birthday Numbers, 13
Black Water/Blue Wind, 20
Blizzard, 161
Blizzard, 192
Bob Broderson's Song of the Wheel, 193
Brolgas, 204
Builders, 14
Burning of Applewood, A, 143
Caroline, 334
Catullus in a Datsun, 342
Ceremonial Song for the Cleansing of the Wind, 18

Chain of Saws, A, 324
Cockatoos, 203
Colonel Cheeseman's Commencement Party, 105
Concord, 67
Contraries: December, 75
'Correspondances', 235
Cousin Jock, 336
Crocodiles Who Stayed Too Long, The, 258
Dawn in California, 145
Dentist at Work, 134
Detail of an Estrangement, 72
Dogwood, 16
Dung Beetle, 146
Ecstasy of Karmstad Karleson, The, 107
Elegy for a Staring Boy, 325
Even Stevens, 336
Falling, 311
Field-Notes for the War Against England, 37
First Day, The, 66
For Hélène, 235
For Raman, 22
For Rolfe, Coming Home, 24
Four Songs for Children, 182
Fourteenth Honeymoon at the Cameron Hotel, 123
Francesca, 176
From Basho's 81 Poems on the Moods and Modes of the Pigeon, 269
From the Japanese, 237
General, 35
Geoffrey, 173
Gift for My Daughters, A, 310
Great Masters, 319
Hands, 333
Hanging Pigeon, 191
Hangover Poem, 253
Happy Day Among the Elephant People, 257
Hawk on a Burnt Pole, 17
He Rebukes His Underwear, 258
He Recapitalues/Forecast the Stages of His Life, 254
Her Rationale, 117
Here, 155
Hideaway, 186
Hired Man's Retrospect of Winter, The, 136
His Afterthought, 117
Horse Latitudes, The, 188

Hot Day in Kansas City, A, 113
House in the Bush, The, 65
I and Franko, 183
In My Freshman Year, 33
In Small, 322
In the Painted Ocean, 189
Interview with Basho, An, 264
Invention, An, 122
Island Weather of the Newly Betrothed, The, 118
It Just Isn't Fair, 182
It's Over Again, 185
Japanese Windbell's, The, 191
Jim Busby's Rune at Cider Time, 190
Justice Barrie and His Mistress, 338
Kids, 306
Kind of Love Poem, A, 19
King of the Gallery, 176
Kookaburra Kanon, 201
Last Evening, 150
Late Breakfast, 258
Late Summer, 73
Leavings, 341
Legs, 34
Leichardt in the Desert, 135
Lines for a Teacher, 108
Lions, etc., 347
Little Midnight Elegy, A, 25
Love Poem after Heavy Snow, 26
Lovers, 117
Macropeus Giganteus, 206
Magpies, 205
Man Dead, A, 104
Man in the Train, 126
Man with a Phone, 36
Married Song, 121
Masters of Haiku, 237
Mild June Day, A, 70
Minnesota Winterdrive, 259
Morning Music, 73
Mother and Dad at Ninety-Three, 351
Nine for a Wasp at Lunchtime, 164
North, 115
Not Quite Ithaka, 151
Not Thinking Now, 313

Note from the Bridge, A, 187
Oenone's Jingle, 182
Old Ted, 175
Olof Andersson's Rune, 128
Opal Miners, 132
Otters at Battle Lake, 316
Past Sixty-five by a Month or More, 11
Piero, Painting, 127
Pirra in Deep Winter, 309
Pleasures, 307
Points in a Journey, 65
Post Graduate, 133
Postlude: A Sentimental Elegy, 267
Profondeurs at 2.a.m., 353
Quarrel, 318
Questions for Oenone, 312
Quick Shadow, 253
Railroad Tanka, 259
Red Fox in Winter, 326
Refusing Song, 71
Reply to the Grammarians, 253
Revenge, 305
Rock Lizard, 17
Sage Who Came By, The, 257
Scribbled in the Back of *The Origin of Species*, 321
Sense of Falling, The, 149
Seriously, 332
Seven Dream Poems, 260
Seven Thoughts on Poetry, 307
Single Handed, 112
Single Tree, A, 232
Six Little Songs on Time, 184
Sketch for an Aesthetic, 254
Sleepless in Florence, 74
Snail-Tracks, 354
So Quietly, 111
Song from a Play, 127
Song of a Lecherous Man, 119
Song of the Central Tree, 195
Song of the Earth, 49
Songs from the Drifting House, 187
Songs of Lara and the Bellarine, 173
Spring Poems from the Kokinshu, 240
Squatters, The, 229

Summer Poem, 153
Surf at Whitnaby, The, 124
T-Shirt Poems, 344
Thank You, Pythagoras, 331
Fallow Season, The, 161
Three Chants for Voice and Didjeridu, 178
Three Love Poems, 237
Time of Gold, A, 67
Tomb of an Apostle, 232
Town and Country Suite, A, 191
Trades, 67
Transatlantic Versions of Rimbaud's '*Ma Bohème*', 231
Traveling Toward the *Vache Qui Pue* River, 256
Two Poems by Théo Léger, 232
Two Popular Songs, 185
Two Spanish Pieces, 73
Two Variations on a Ground, 162
Two Women, 103
Uncle Jack, 101
Under the Lime-Tree, 233
Vita: Minnesota Fall, 12
Warm Day in January, A, 192
Water Man, The, 79
Wave Cave, 179
Wayne Comes Back from Utah, 21
Wedding Song, 312
Wedding Song, 44
When the Irish Bulls Rolled Over, 287
Where Do Birds Go, 183
White Song, 187
White Wave, 211
White-Faced Heron, 202
Widow of Wild Dog Creek, A, 174
Wife Waiting, 130
Wimmera Snake-Time, 346
Winemaker's Winter Song, The, 177
Winter Canticle, 27
Word in December, A, 162
Words for *The Immigrants*, 314
Worlds, 68
Young Bears in an Orchard, 155

INDEX OF FIRST LINES

(First lies of individual poems are shown in roman type. First lines of sections or smaller poems in sequences are in italics.)

A cat's eye glares at me, sharp green, 184
A chessboard, 261
A costive artist is a howling contradiction, 324
A day of cloud and the grey Hawkesbury, 66
A day of pine-smells and early crickets, 105
A ketch heels, 344
A line of soldiers plunges down the mountain, 261
A man is dead, one whom we almost knew, 104
A quick dart and an abrupt stop, 164
A rope of smoke winds slow, 126
A shock of fragrant almond-blossom, should it persist, 59
A story then, 165
A thimbleful of the hard stuff, 101
A wave of early snow, 187
All day we push this beaded wall, 184
All my life I have been afraid of death, 263
An old train jammed in a box, bogey broken, 310
As an awkward kid I prayed beside this bed, 311
As far as eye can see, 240
As the April sunlight drew the last, 194
As the mother of grain taught men to plow, 57
Bad-tempered and disgusted, 188
Basho is dead and his ideas, 263
Bean curd, 258
Because I ate three Eskimos for tea, 182
Because my father told me, No, 12
Because of a pain that erupted, and the heat, 74
Buy gloves, and, 338
Chopin winding down again, 25
Climb into the high bed from the oak footstool, 123
Daddy, I love you Deliberately, 182
Dog yaps, 269
Dozing at noon, 237
Drove up here, 346
Dumb bastards, living down here — just for bits of fire, 132
Each night there's been a queer complaint in the door, 72
Early springtime mists, 240
Exactly at four o'clock, 145
Ezra Pound, 354
Faster than, 345

365

Father, blubber, grease body, 257
Five years, and still the ash-trees and the ferns, 174
Flies doze on, 344
Fortnightly, 258
Fric, fric, 204
Glide always beneath your meaning, 207
Great masters, 319
Great walls of it, seething in, fast, from Mexico, 311
Green burns down, 344
Gymnnorhina, 205
Hacks at our faces, a low cloud, 192
Hard rain clacks around, 187
He carry no wings, 206
Hearing your absence now in every room, 19
Here is a man examining his hands, 112
Here we are in our hot boots, the fire, 143
Here you are, 333
Hey, Jack!, 201
His brother, 295
His home a 336
Home by myself in my draughty house, 151
How does the swallow find what skein, 184
How does the word banana mean, 165
How many one-legged soldiers have marched for two-legged kings, 34
How would you like a galoshes breakfast, 183
I am a knockabout man of little learning, 253
I am in bed with a harlot, 260
I am rowing a huge black bull across the lake, 260
I am walking very slowly across Minnesota, 256
I climbed through the sharkproof window, 186
I did not choose to make this westward journey, 135
I find you now, in everything that lives, 230
I have been grave all afternoon, 70
I have come, 37
I have this disease: three-letter word, 133
I hope death, 347
I just goofed off, fists jammed in my levis, 231
I kicked a rock from the canyon's lip, 184
I knew him quite well in his younger days, 263
I loved you once: sometimes my love can still, 230
I met a man who lived too long, 257
I said to them that this was all the time hardly even, 259
I shall strut for you, I shall isolate, 166
I step into our bedroom, 241

I tell you, wood, 195
I walk the gleaming rails, 259
I walk through the long suburbs questioning, 259
I want to get next to my brother, 66
I wish at least that I could die tonight, 267
I woke this morning thick in the head, 193
I write a perfect poem, 261
I, Olof Erik Andersson, 128
Ice on the wind, 16
Ice-wind slaps my eyes and colored suns, 236
Icicle, 345
If a man is intent on writing, 254
If I were wind, 325
In a few days it's going to snow, 234
In my freshman year the fury of Vietnam, 33
Is it the wasp sings at my ear, 164
It's an afternoon of birds in a low sky, 70
It's five long summers since my old grandmother died, 236
It's light, the long egg-tomatoes, 65
I'm leaving now, and then packed up his bag, 103
Jealousy, 354
Jenny Holliday's gliding over the river, 185
Jumping again, 191
Just as my hand goes round, 155
Just now I heard the screech owl, 129
Kelpies dodge, 336
Knowing all that, 53
Let new-cut fields go fallow, rest them, 54
Like sailors, hauling homeward through, 59
Look at the red fox sliding under the wind, 27
Love occurs, 354
Margaret, 341
Mist at the end of pencils, 309
Mister, if I could illustrate this moment, 134
Morning flares, 344
Must've been the sake, 253
My father whacked me with a piece of wood, 305
My father, 14
My father's, 351
My friend Verconi keeps a black machine that squats, 150
My wings fester with light, 17
Nature's a temple where each living column, 235
Never move my tail though the sun bang down, 178
Long one booming under our boots, 179

No one, 317
Nonsense to say it's a kind of music, 127
Sweet curve of thigh, the neural itch, 127
Not like a ticker tape that clicks out minutes in, 79
Not thinking now, you step through the pane, 313
Now to implements and tools which all, 58
Out early. Just as we round the channel-buoy, 20
Out there, skinny pheasants rattle the cornstalks, 325
Past sixty-five by a month or more, 11
Pearl-shell light, 18
Piss off!, 203
Rising, we strap time on our wrists, 184
River split, we heard the crack, 192
Sixty-five, soon sixty-six, 13
So I cleared off, fists in my battered jeans, 231
Some day, after your kind, you'll die, 35
Someone poured cold water on my toe, 254
Something denser perhaps. Than bits of snow, 75
Something is singing in the woman, 73
Sometimes I catch that white face, 166
Sometimes, especially when the wind, 167
Somewhere out in the night, 188
Soon we'll be, 332
Spiders spin, 345
Stand here, 180
Strolling in the garden, 253
Stuck, 289
Sunlight strikes across a page of, 321
Surge like white water round, 306
Susan and Billy and Helen and me, 147
Tat tvam asi, 257
That scrawny bird twitching on a cracked wing, 162
That winter past, troubled by the death fear, 136
The ball of tumbleweed that danced on the empty air, 312
The best poems walk toward us as lovers do, 307
The bowl of a brilliantly lacquered lute, 260
The day was still as honey in a bowl, 155
The drift climbs them higher and higher, 161
Think of that disenchantment, that sharp breaking, 162
The edge of the city turns over in sleep, 326
The eye by the way of the field mouse to the comma, 264
The figure forms a cross, take a stick and draw it, 115
The man who woke me with his tuneless whistle, 73
The night you, 334

The poet Basho is dead, 262
The same wave bowled me over, 213
The screech owl speaks again, and we are night, 224
The skin of the lake hardens again, 316
The winds are more predictable in summer, 118
The yellow tractor, 322
Then, turning, she said: Let's make love, 117
There is a moment in a wineglass, 168
There must be someone breathing here, 113
There was this message, 249
There's a ghost of bad music, 318
These drifting afternoons, while others, 119
These shadows moving over new-ploughed land, 161
They measured the chosen one against the granite slab, 232
They patched my face with, 202
They're harvesting. A yellow tractor, 222
Thinking of him again, 237
This is a time of dangerous gold, 67
This late jazz, 353
This little, 331
This the hour that seems to lose the clock, 130
This time I am inside a jasmine flower, 260
Three times, full circle, 218
Thrums in his midden-mound, 146
Times like that, 57
Today old Ted is eighty-four, 175
Two photographs pinned on my wall, 68
Two whole days, in white explosions, 26
Under roof-trees where bantams listen, like snow-, 107
Under the lime-tree near the meadow, 232
Vinnie, 122
Wakening early to a whiff, 184
Watch out for geese and cranes who scrabble, 56
Then came the age of traps and springes, 56
Wayne comes back from Utah with dark stories, 21
We are farther from England than the moon, 314
We are his, 339
We go along, sometimes for decades, 36
Wet midsummers, clear, 55
We've eaten well, and drowse, 189
What are the high crows telling us, 17
What are you doing, down there, head hanging, 124
What came of fire was fire, 46
What in your mild latitude, 312

What makes your corn shoot high, 49
In first spring, 52
What moves, is what I say, 176
Whatever the fig meant, 258
When a dancer spins so fast the space around her liquefies, 307
When all your choices tightened about you, 24
When Basho awoke in his bed, 262
When Geoffrey plays the flute, 173
When I first felt the white wind slide, 177
When I'm back, 342
When I'm gone, 355
When maybe a sparrow clicked his nail, 71
When the screech owl speaks, 215
When you are old and these words cross your tongue, 235
When you thrust out from a bewildered waking, 121
Where do birds when they sleep, 183
While Daddy chops and Mummy hums, 176
Who gave mouth-to-mouth to the drowning, 22
Who this hand that choked the bird, 191
Who would have thought that you, so quietly, 111
Why are your hands so grease-black, mine, 67
Wind-bitten neighbor's and their wives, 190

Wolf-black, spindle-shanked, green rings round their eyes, 229
You buried your mother, 153
You have to get up early, 131
You must excuse me, there's a place not far, 167
You told my daughter what, 108
Your dawn-call, 354
Your walking here has made no sound at all, 44
You're dozing there, four hundred feet, 149

Prints by Karin Calley
Plants of the Australian southern tablelands

Acacia, 7
Dianella revoluta, 29
Microlaena stipoides [Weeping grass seeds], 47
Vittadinia, 61
Elymus scaber [Wheat grass], 77
Acacia and *Myoporum floribundum*, 97
Dichelechne, 139
Bothriochloa macra [Redleg grass], 157
Acacia, 169
Themeda australus [Kangaroo grass], 197
Juncus acutus, 209
Dichelachne, 225
Myoporum floribundum, 243
Dianella revoluta, 301
Austrostipa bigeniculata, 327

Keith Harrison was born in Victoria, Australia, and educated at the University of Melbourne. After teaching three years in Australia he began a long odyssey which took him first to England, where he was a freelance journalist, broadcaster, reviewer and Tutor in English in the Extra-mural of the University of London. In the late sixties he spent a short year at the Writer's Workshop at the University of Iowa, then took up a lectureship in English at York University, Toronto. From there he moved to Minnesota to teach in the English department at Carleton College, and remained there as Professor of English and Writer in Residence for almost three decades.

He has published twelve collections of poetry, the latest being *The Complete Basho Poems* (2002) and a verse translation of *Sir Gawain and the Green Knight* (Oxford World's Classics, 1998). His poems, plays, and translations have been published and broadcast in many places throughout the English-speaking world and he is represented in more than a dozen anthologies in Australia, England, and America. Fellowships and awards for his literary work have been granted by (among others) the University of Melbourne, the British Arts Council, the Canada Council, and the Bush Foundation of Minnesota.

Presently working on several books, including a prismatic memoir called *Not Quite Ithaka*, he divides his time between his old farmhouse in Northfield, Minnesota and various locales in Australia. He is blessed by two daughters, two grandchildren, and many friends on the three continents which have shaped his days and his imagination.

www.ingramcontent.com/pod-product-compliance
Lightning Source LLC
Chambersburg PA
CBHW081935170426
43202CB00018B/2926